Baa Baa Black Sheep

Read this poem with a grown-up.

Baa baa black sheep
Have you any wool?
Yes sir, yes sir, three bags full.

One for the master
And one for the dame
And one for the little boy
Who lives down the lane.

Do you know this rhyme? Perhaps you have a toy sheep you can use to act it out!

I Look at these shapes. Draw over them with your pencil.

a 

b 

c 

d 

II Answer these questions.

a What colour is the sheep in the poem? Colour the sheep below the right colour.

b How many bags of wool does the sheep have? Draw them here.

Looking for *o*

The letter *o* is round like a ball.

I **The letter *o* is hiding in each of these groups of pictures. Draw a circle round the *o* shaped picture.**

a

c

e

g

b

d

f

h

II **Join the dots to draw an *o* shape and finish each picture.**

a
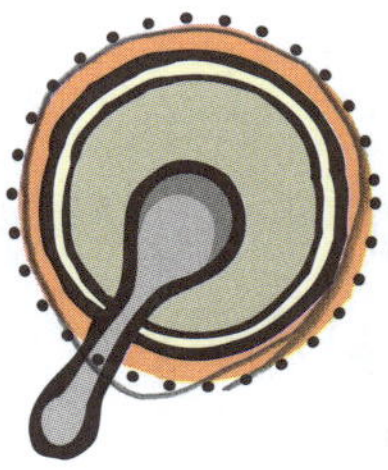

c

e
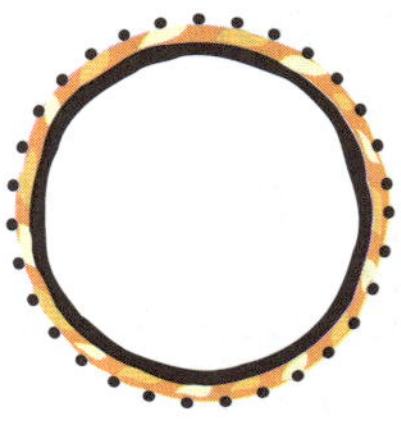

g
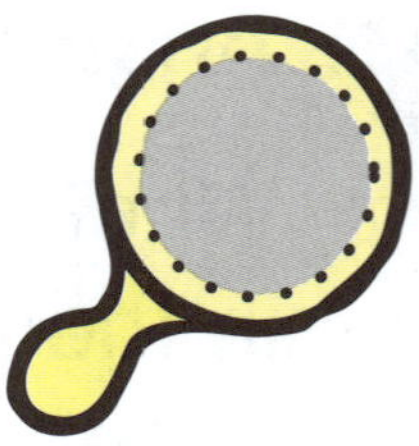

b
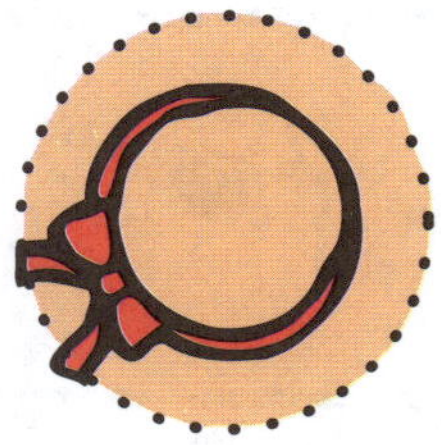

d

f

h

Looking for *s*

The letter *s* looks like a wiggly worm.

I Find the letter *s* in the pictures and colour the picture in.

a 

c 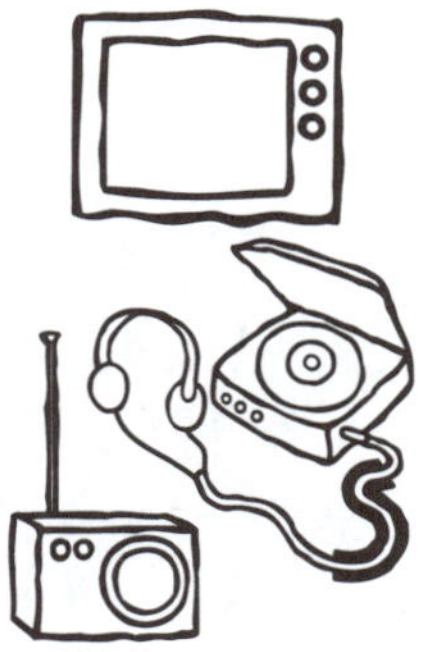

e 

g 

b 

d 

f 

h 

II Circle the letter *s* in each word.

a spoon
b sweet
c bus
d house
e shed
f seal
g past
h ask
i saw

Looking for *i*

The letter **i** is easy to write. It is a line with a dot at the top.

I **The itchy iguana is having ideas! Write the letter *i* on each idea bubble.**

II **There is a letter *i* hiding in each of these words. Find them and draw a circle round each one.**

a

i n k

b

r i n g

c

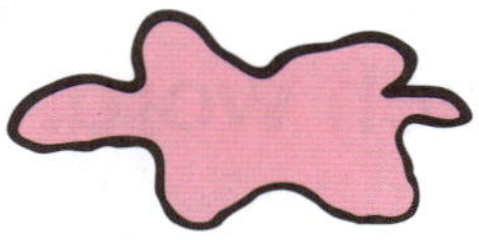

p i n k

d

g i r l

e

i m p

f

p i g

Writing shapes

Writing is hard work, so you can practise by drawing patterns. They help you to make the shapes you need to write letters.

You need round shapes

lines

and tails and hooks

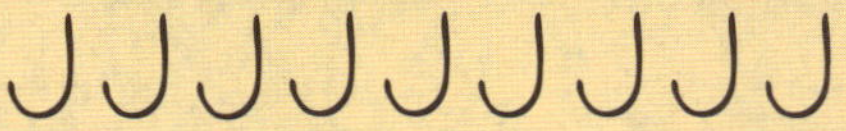

I Draw over these patterns.

a 

b 

c 

d 

II Draw over these letters.

a 

b 

c 

d 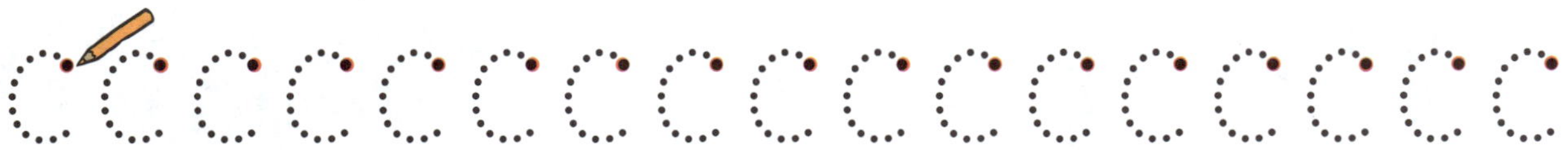

Where am I?

Pussy cat, pussy cat
Where have you been?
I've been to London to
visit the Queen.

Pussy cat, pussy cat
What did you there?
I frightened a little
mouse under the chair!

I **Under, on or in front of? Finish the picture to match the sentence.**

a The mouse is under the chair.

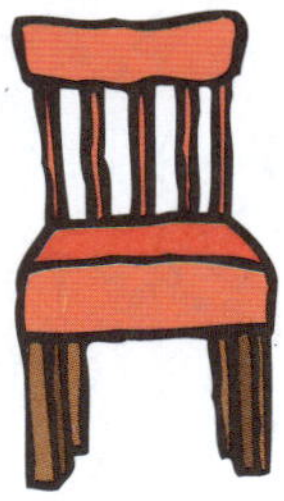

b The crown is on the Queen's head.

c The cat is in front of the mouse.

II **Draw these.**

a Draw a spider under the table.

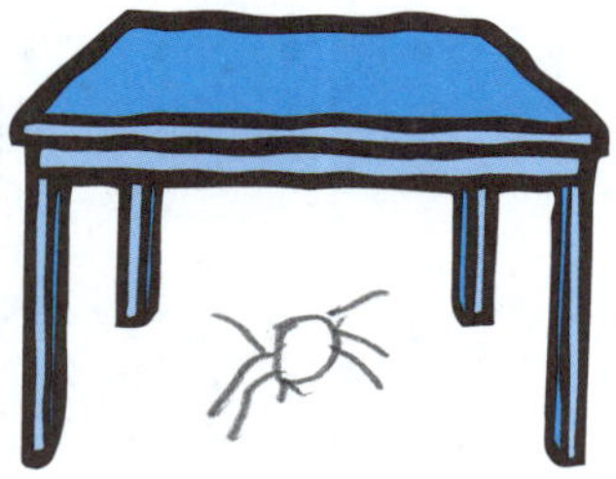

b Draw a bee on the flower.

The right order

It is important to do things in the right order.

I Which thing should you do first? Put 1 and 2 in the boxes to show the right order.

a [2] dry yourself — [1] get out of the bath

b [1] eat dinner — [2] eat pudding

c [1] put on gloves — [2] go out in the cold

d [2] brush your hair — [1] get out of bed

e [1] go to bed — [2] brush your teeth

II Put the pictures in the right order. Write 1 to 4 in the boxes.

a

[1]

b

[4]

c

[2]

d

[3]

Looking for *n*

Look at this letter.
It is an *n*.

I **Draw a line to join the words that begin with *n* to the big letter *n*.**

II **Ask a grown-up to help you cut out some pictures from a magazine that begin with *n*. Stick them in the space below.**

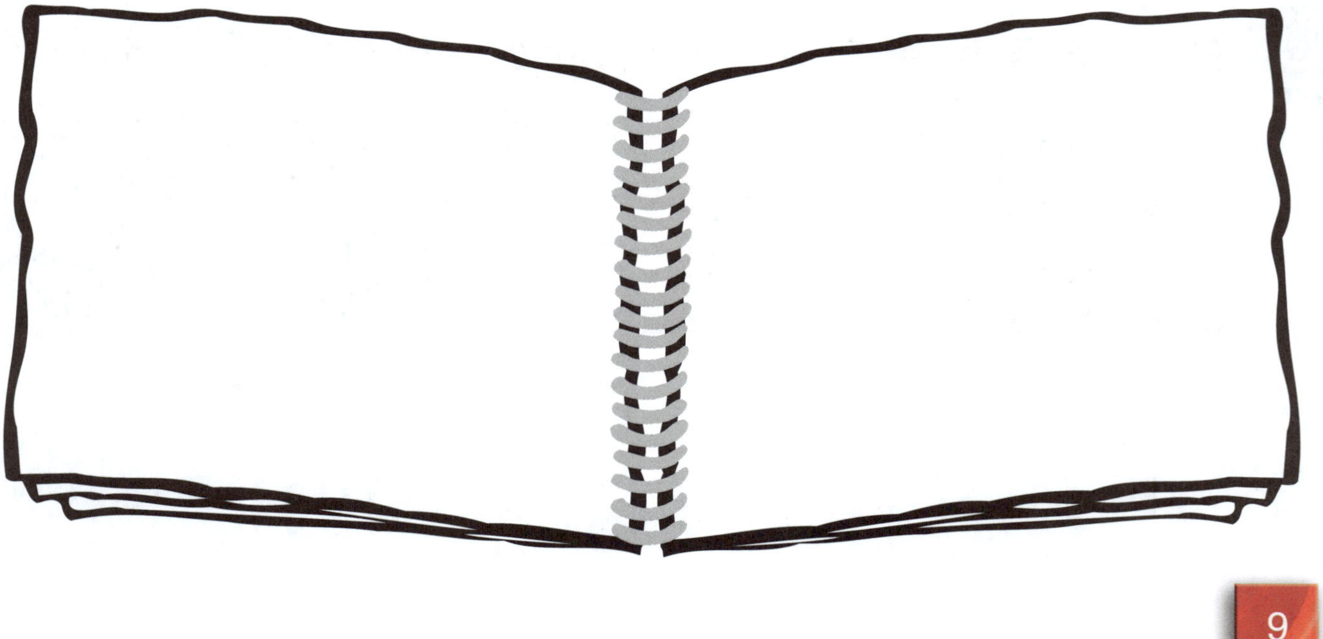

Hearing *s*

The letter *s* sounds like a snake hissing.

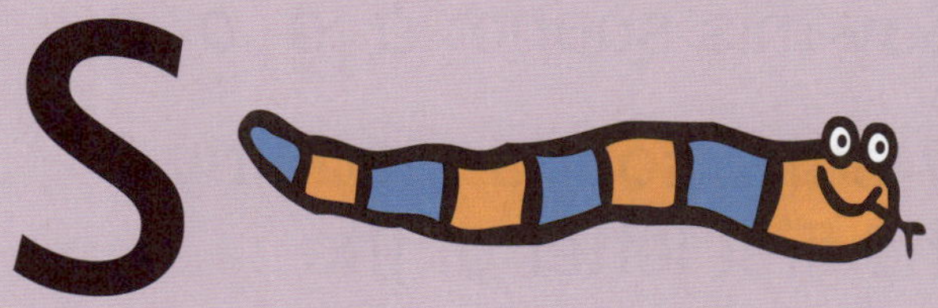

I

Ask a grown-up to read these words out loud. Which ones start with *s*? Circle the word.

a sea air rock

b pepper salt mustard

c cat dog snake

d egg sausage bacon

e sandwich cake biscuit

f funny silly naughty

g sand pebble weed

h pebble starfish crab

i rain wind sun

j toilet bath sink

II

Ask a grown-up to read these words. Listen carefully. Tick the words that end in *s*.

a hands ☐

b toes ☐

c face ☐

d legs ☐

e arm ☐

f ears ☐

g knee ☐

h foot ☐

i ankles ☐

j hair ☐

k apples ☐

l seaside ☐

Hearing a

Say this sound: *a a a a*

a is the sound made by the first letter of the alphabet.

I **Draw a line to join the words that begin with *a* to the big letter *a*.**

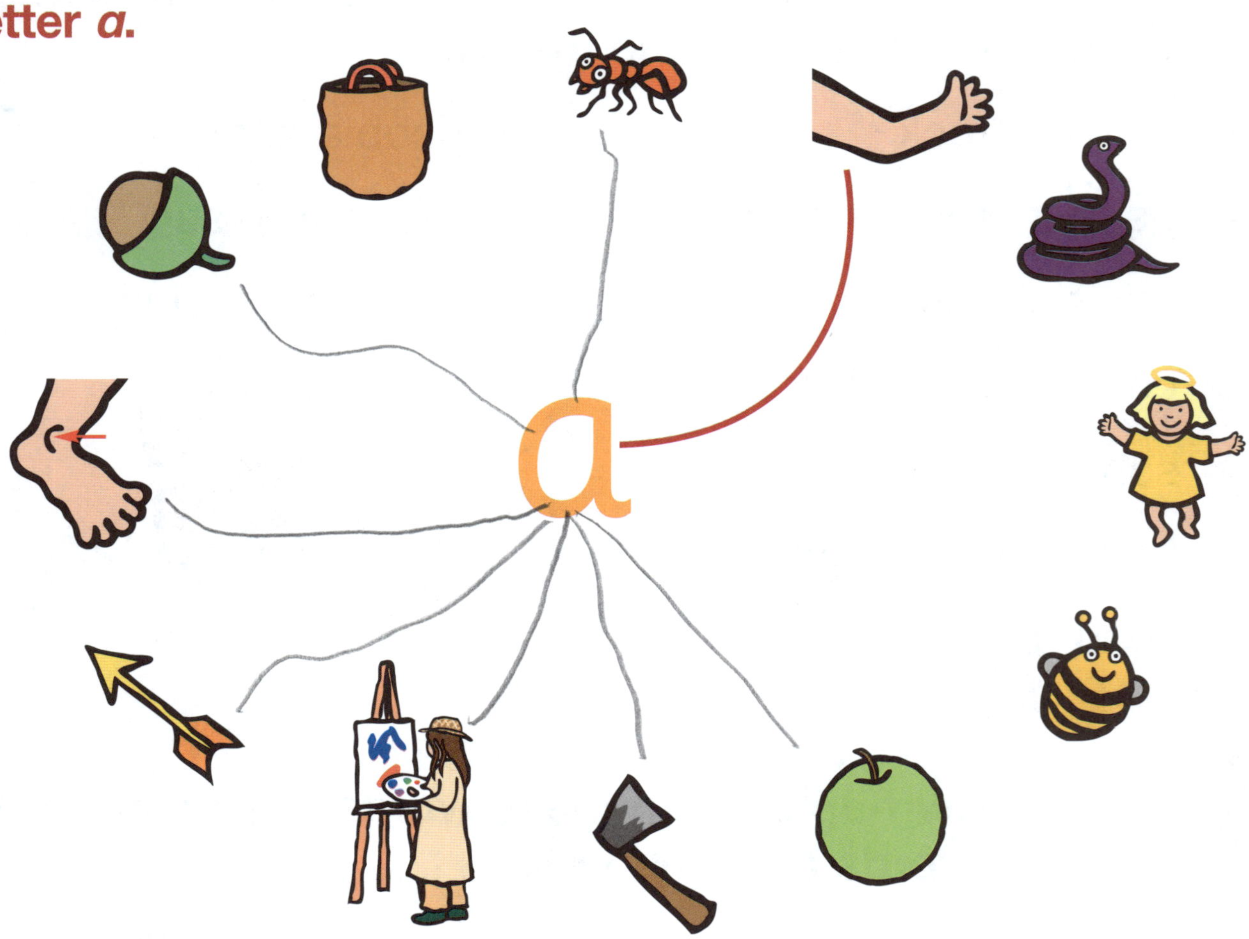

II **Ask a grown-up to read these words out loud. Circle the ones that have an *a* sound in the middle.**

a	man	met	d	mat	met	g	fan	fin	j	lap	lip
b	pin	pan	e	sat	set	h	did	dad	k	pot	pat
c	bin	ban	f	bit	bat	i	rat	rut	l	run	ran

The North Wind Doth Blow

Read this poem with a grown-up.

The north wind doth blow
And we shall have snow
And what will the robin
do then, poor thing?

He'll sit in the barn
And keep himself warm
And hide his head under
his wing, poor thing!

The north wind doth blow
And we shall have snow
And what will the dormouse
do then, poor thing?

Rolled up in a ball
In his nest snug and small
He'll sleep 'til warm weather
comes in, poor thing!

I Answer the questions to see how carefully you have listened to the poem!

a What is blowing? Draw a picture of it in this box.

b What weather is coming? Draw the weather here.

II Make up a story about the robin and the dormouse. How could they help each other to keep warm? Use the boxes to draw pictures to tell your story. Then tell the story to a grown-up.

The alphabet

The letters of the alphabet are always in this order.

a b c d e f g h i j k l m n
o p q r s t u v w x y z

I **Follow the alphabet and join the dots with a pencil.**

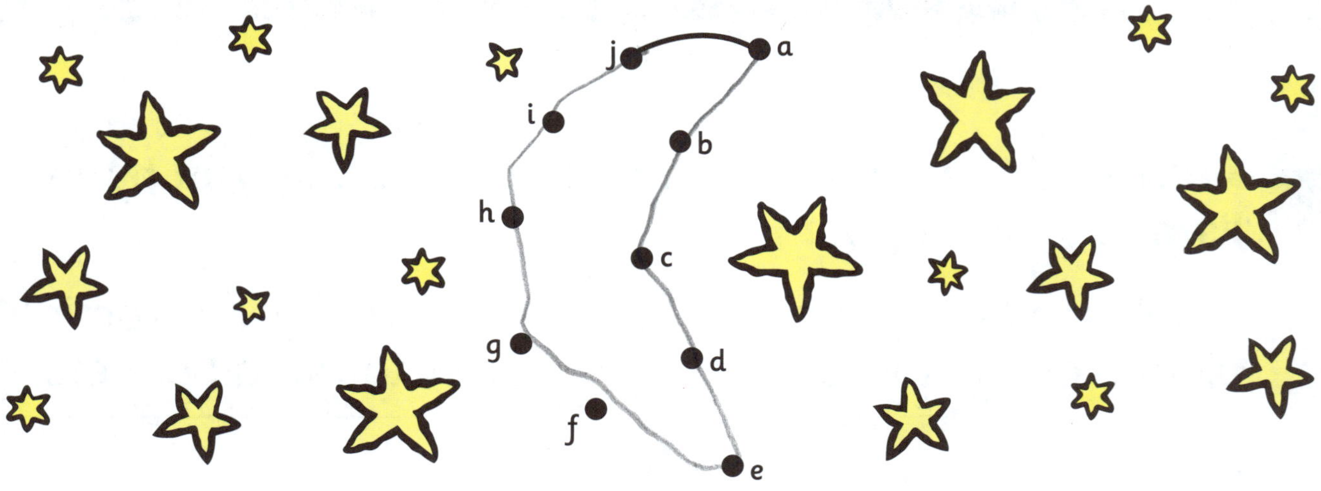

The picture is of the ___ ___ ___ ___.

II **Write the letter that comes next.**

a a b c	**d** j k L	**g** s t u
b d e f	**e** m n o	**h** v w x
c g h i	**f** p q r	**i** x y z

What is the sound?

Each letter of the alphabet makes a sound.

I Draw a line to join the animals to their beginning sounds.

a 

c 

e 

g 

z r c d f s m l

b 

d 

f 

h 

II Circle the sounds these toys start with.

a t b g 

c m f d 

e h r z 

b f p b 

d h s r 

f f l s 

Days of the week

Every day has its own special name. They also have a special order.

Monday Tuesday Wednesday Thursday
Friday Saturday Sunday

I **Draw a picture to show what you do on the different days of the week.**

Monday Friday Saturday Sunday

II **Go over the words with your pencil and write the days of the week.**

Monday Friday
Tuesday Saturday
Wednesday Sunday
Thursday

Looking for *p*

The letter *p* is made of a stick with a ball joined to the top.

I Find the *p* on each picture and trace over it.

a 

b 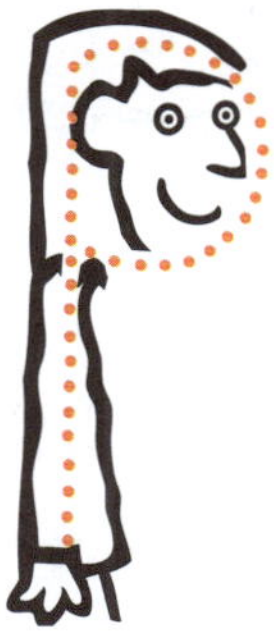

c 

d 

e 

f 

g 

h 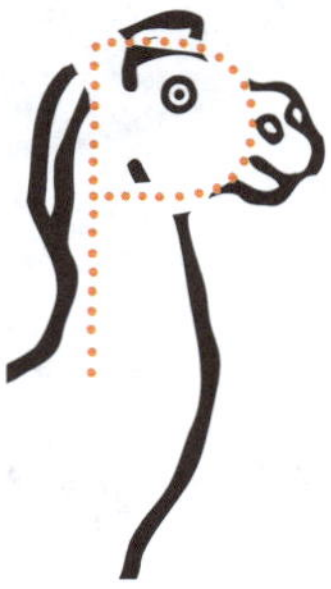

II Circle the word in each set that starts with the letter *p*.

a part talk what

b now past ask

c wash pit like

d go fit pot

e will name pop

f mug pea tap

More about the alphabet

Do you remember the order of the alphabet?

a b c d e f g h i j k l m n

o p q r s t u v w x y z

I This alphabet has some letters missing. Fill them in.

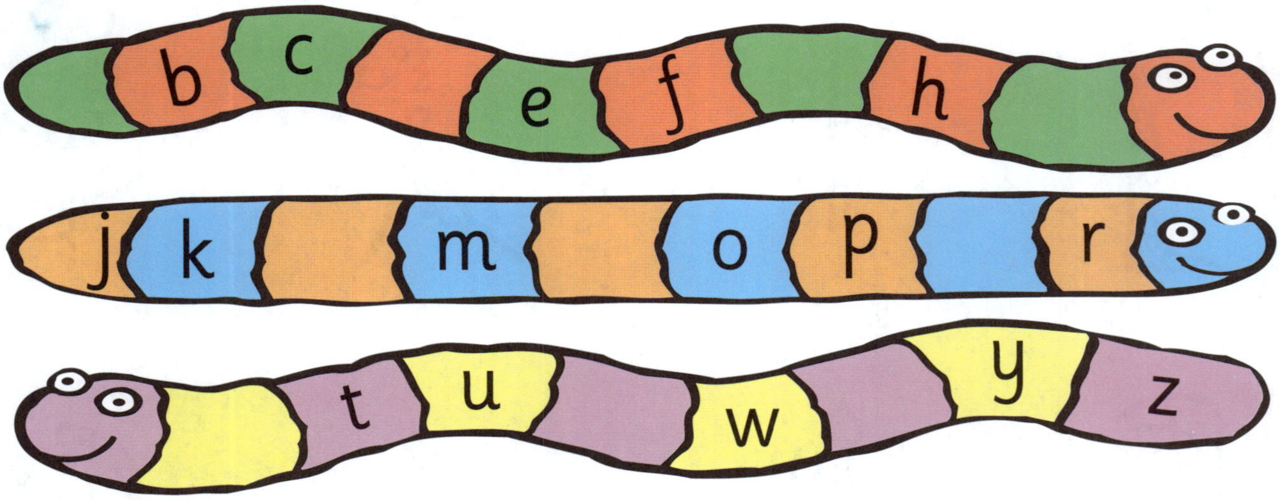

II Join the dots, starting at the letter *a* and going through the letters of the alphabet to find which sweet the picture is of.

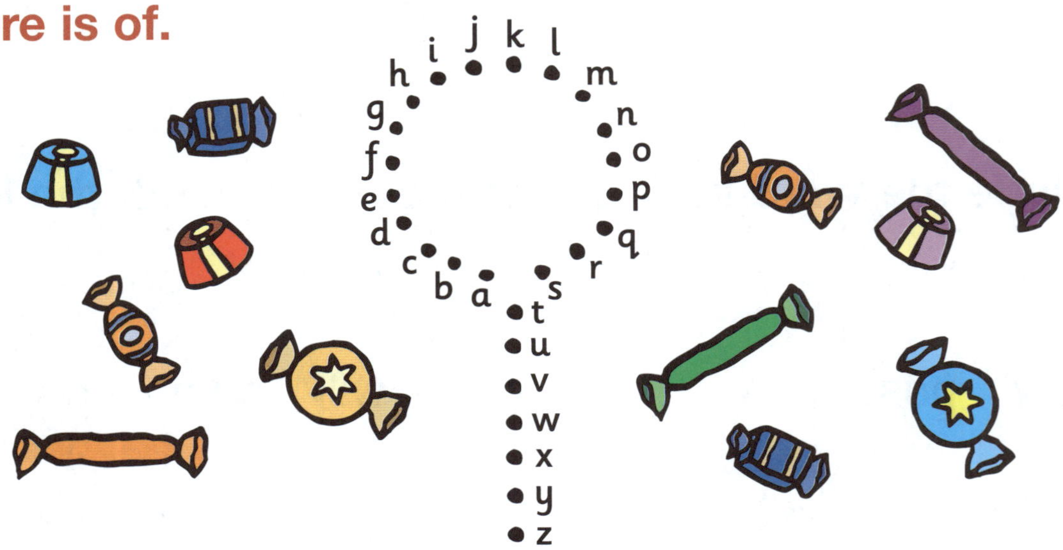

The picture is of a ___ ___ ___ ___ ___.

Months of the year

Every month has its own special name. We use a capital letter when we write them.

I

Talk about the pictures with a grown-up. Then match the pictures to the right months.

a 

b 

c 

d 

e 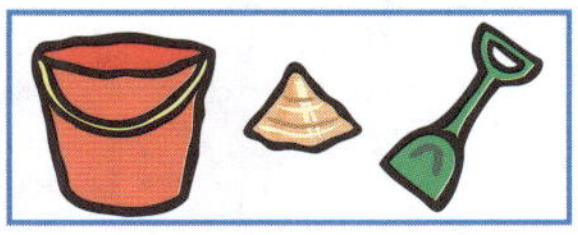

f 

January
February
March
April
May
June
July
August
September
October
November
December

g 

h 

i 

j 

k 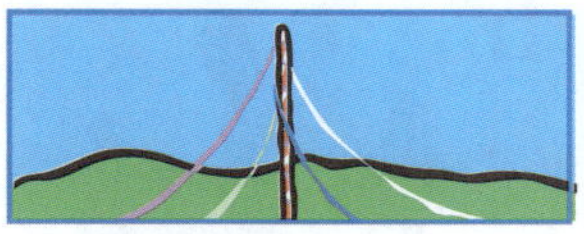

l 

II

Write over the words below with your pencil to write the months of the year.

January	May	September
February	June	October
March	July	November
April	August	December

Hearing *t*

Say this sound: *t t t t*

It is made by the letter *t*!

t

tick tick tick tick

I

Say the name of the picture and put a tick ✓ if the word starts with a *t* sound and a cross ✗ if it does not.

a  ☐

c  ☐

e  ☐

g  ☐

b  ☐

d  ☐

f  ☐

h  ☐

II

Circle the things that start with *t*.

All about me

What is your name? Write it here.

____

Do you know all the words for the parts of your body, so you can talk about yourself?

I Finish the words to label the picture. Start at the red dots.

II Draw a line to join the word to the right body part.

a head **b** hand **c** arm **d** leg **e** knee **f** foot **g** eye **h** hair

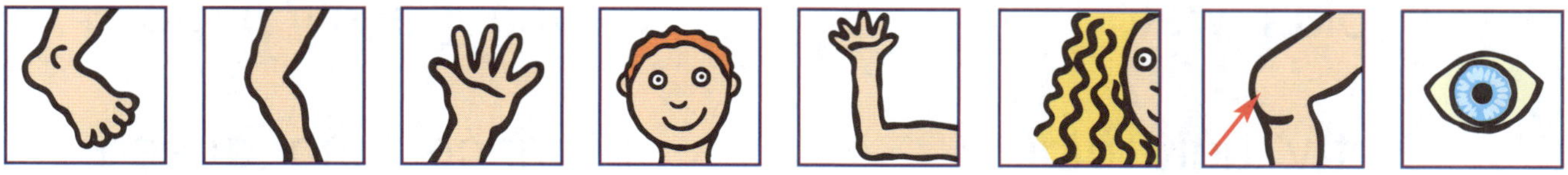

Hearing *p*

When you say the letter *p* it sounds as though you are spitting something out! Have a try.

I **Say what these things are. Which ones start with *p*? Draw a circle round them.**

a
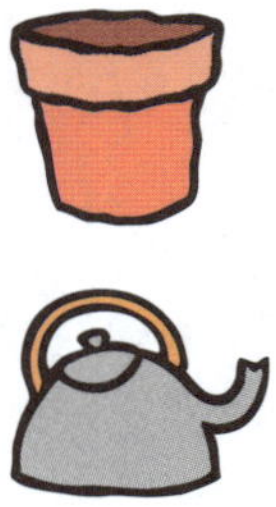

c

e

g

b

d

f
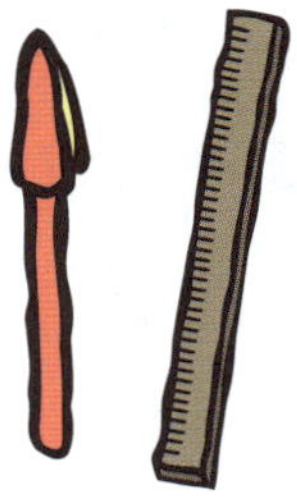

h
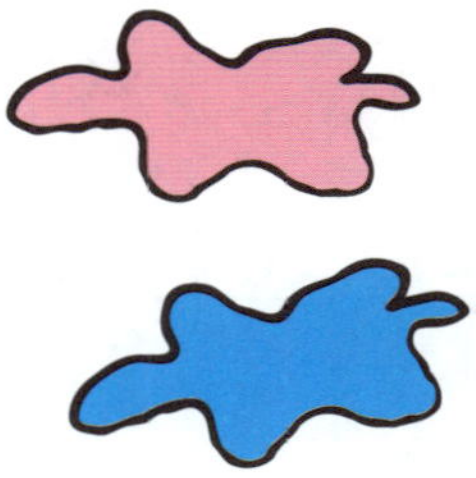

II **Listen to a grown-up read these words. Which words in each group start with *p*? Draw a circle round them.**

a spoon pan kettle

b iron plug plate

c if plan wet

d pretty ugly plain

e pat pin mat

f play no go

g pen pencil paper

h prince king queen

Matching capitals to small letters

Capitals are big letters.
We use them at the
beginning of our names.

I **Draw a line to match the small letters to their capitals.**

c s o z k w p v u x

Z W O X U P K C V S

II **Draw lines to match these letters. They are harder because the capitals look different to their small partners.**

a b d e g h i q r f

F B A G E R H Q I D

The letter *c*

The letter *c* is a curl, like an *o* that has not been finished.

C

cat

I Find the letter *c* in each picture and trace over it.

a 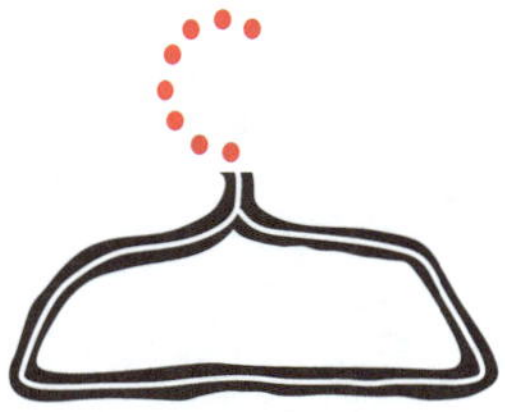

c 

e 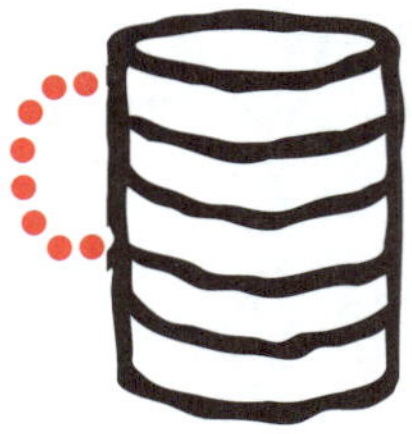

g 

b 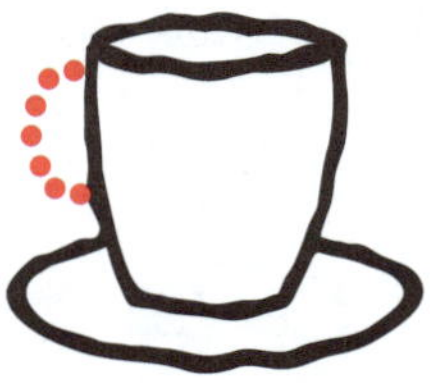

d 

f 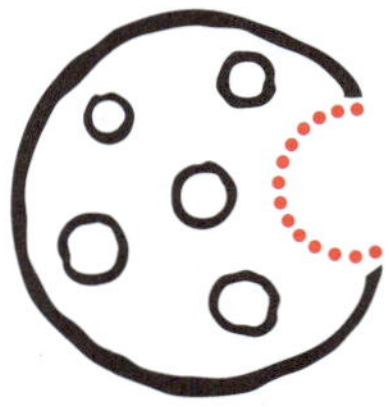

h 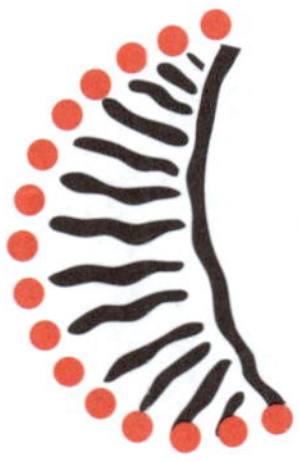

II Draw 5 pictures of things that start with *c*.

Little Bo Peep

Read this poem with a grown-up.

Little Bo Peep
Has lost her sheep
And doesn't know where to find them
Leave them alone
And they'll come home
Wagging their tails behind them.

I Answer these questions about the poem.

a What is the girl called? Write her name here.

____

b What has she lost? Draw them here.

c If she leaves them alone, where will they go? Put a tick under the right picture:

☐ ☐

d What will they wag? Draw it here.

II There are some *ee* sounds in the poem. Find some more *ee* sounds in these words and circle them.

a sheep **c** creep **e** feel **g** peel **i** beet

b sleep **d** feet **f** wheel **h** beer **j** sheet

The seasons

There are four seasons in a year. Each season has its own special name.

spring

summer

autumn

winter

I **Write over these to finish the names of the seasons.**

spring summer

autumn winter

II **Draw a picture for each season.**

The letter b

The letter *b* is a stick with a ball at the bottom.

b 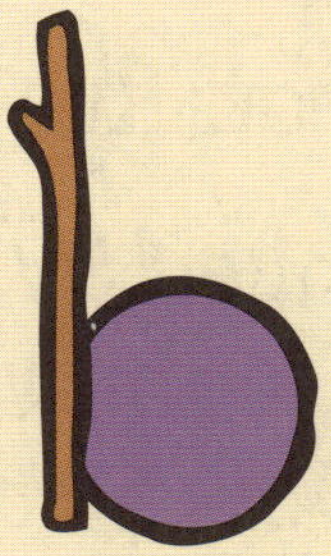

I Find the *b* shapes in each picture and trace over them.

a 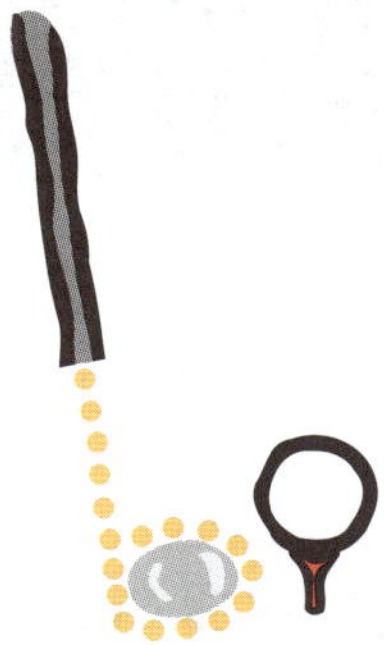

b 

c 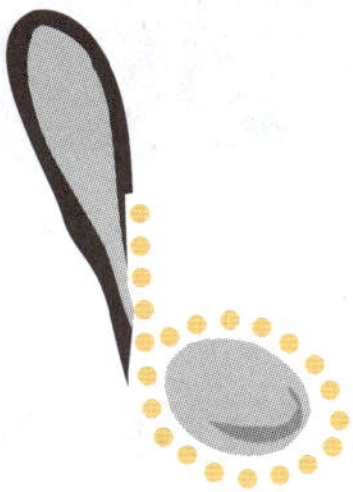

d 

e 

f 

g 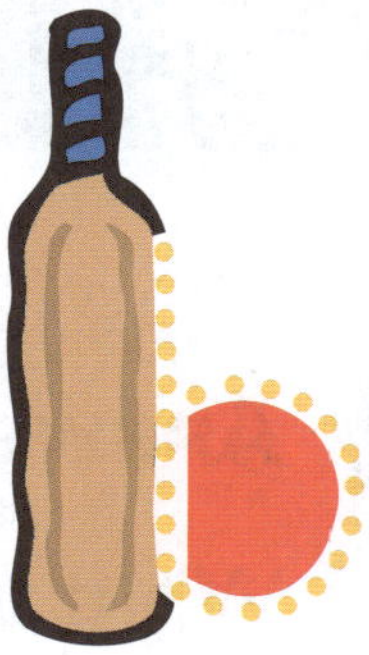

h 

II Colour the things in each pair that start with *b*.

a 

b 

c 

d 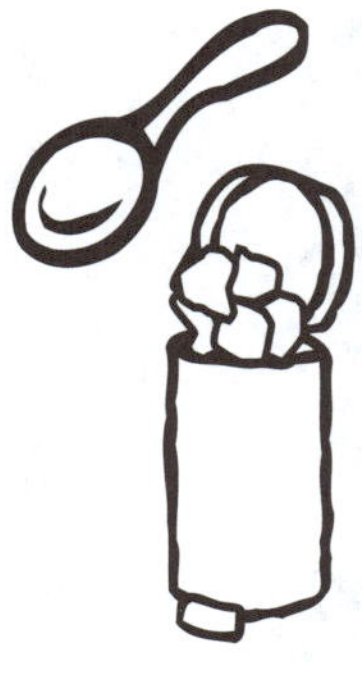

e 

Incey Wincey Spider

Read this poem with a grown-up.

Incey Wincey spider
Climbed up the water spout
Down came the rain
And washed the spider out.
Out came the sunshine
It dried up all the rain
So Incey Wincey spider
Climbed up the spout again.

I Answer these questions about the poem.

a What was the spider climbing? Draw it here.

b What came down the spout? Draw it here.

II Colour all the spiders that have words that start with the sound *sp*.

Finding *i*

The letter *i* sounds like a mouse squeaking.

I **Ask a grown-up to read these words. Draw a circle round the words that start with *i*.**

a ice all but

b pen ink can

c you I me

d think idea plan

e if what when

f well sick ill

g at into mat

h out hill in

i why inch go

j they inside dog

II **Say the names of the things in these pictures. Colour the things that start with *i*.**

a

b

c

d

e

f

Hearing *n*

Say this sound: *n n n n*

Where is your tongue when you say it?

n

nice **n**oodles

I Find the *n* word in each picture and colour it in.

a

b

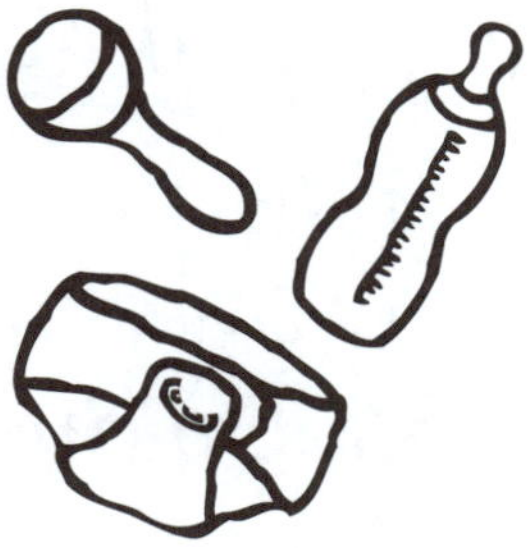

c

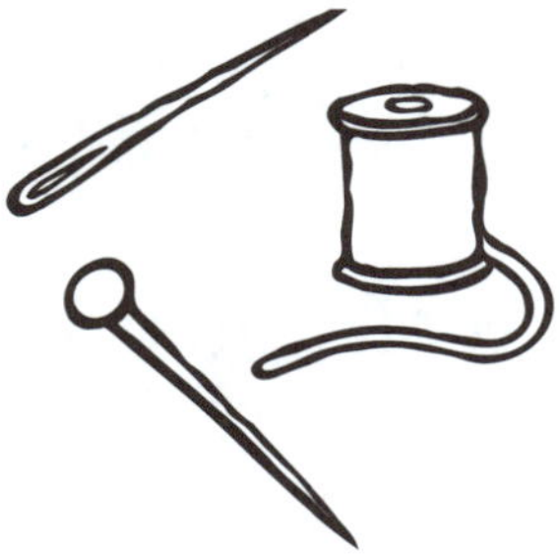

d

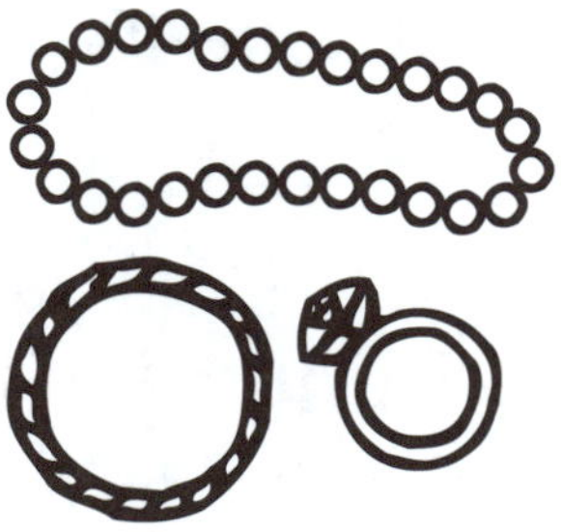

e

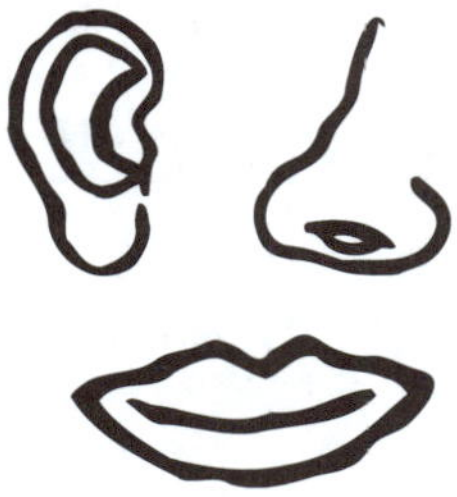

f

II Look at the words in the box. Write the *n* words on the net.

nice yes no nip pip not nib new newt bin nap name

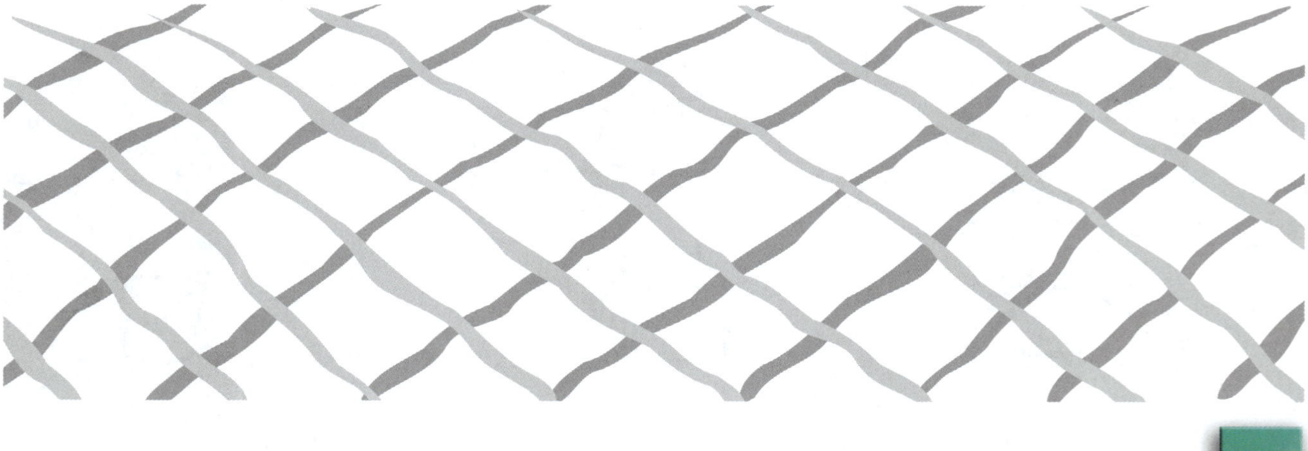

Colour words

Look at these colours.

I Colour the paint pots the right colour.

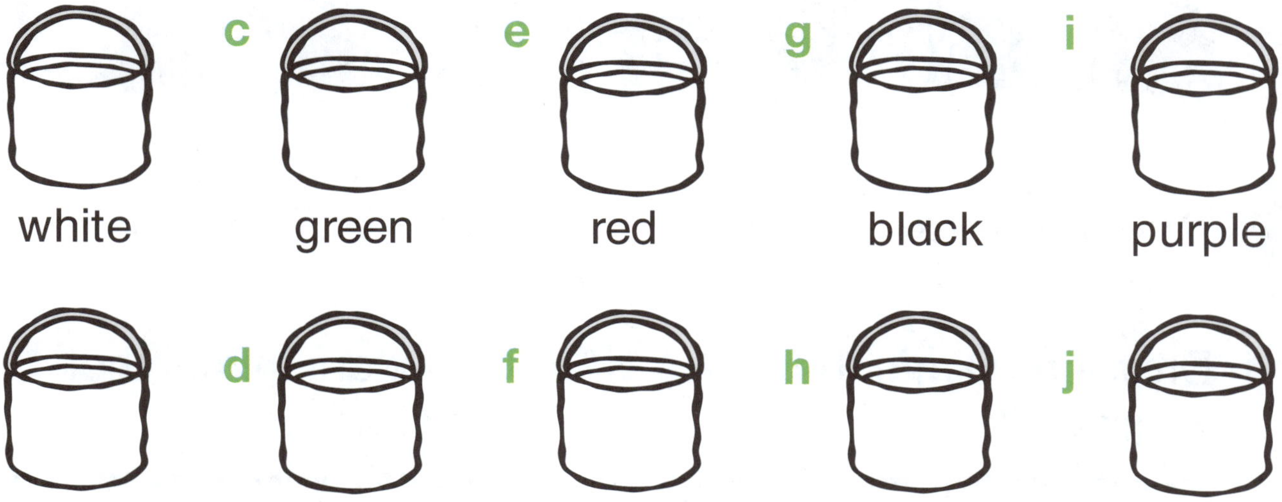

a white
c green
e red
g black
i purple
b blue
d pink
f orange
h brown
j yellow

II Write the colour words. Use the dots to help you.

a A green leaf

b A blue sky

c A red ladybird

d An orange orange

e A brown rabbit

f A pink flower

Animals

Cat starts with the sound *c*.

Mouse starts with *m*.

I **Ask a grown-up to read the animal names to you. Then join the names to the right picture with a line.**

rabbit lion dog parrot monkey snake whale zebra

II **Can you draw an animal alphabet? Draw a picture of an animal for each letter sound.**

a Draw an animal that begins with *a*.

b Draw an animal that begins with *b*.

c Draw an animal that begins with *c*.

d Draw an animal that begins with *d*.

ANSWERS

Page 2
I Check child's drawing.

II a sheep coloured black
b 3 bags

Page 3
I a ball
b plate
c orange
d CD
e pizza
f coin
g glass lenses
h penguin's tummy

II
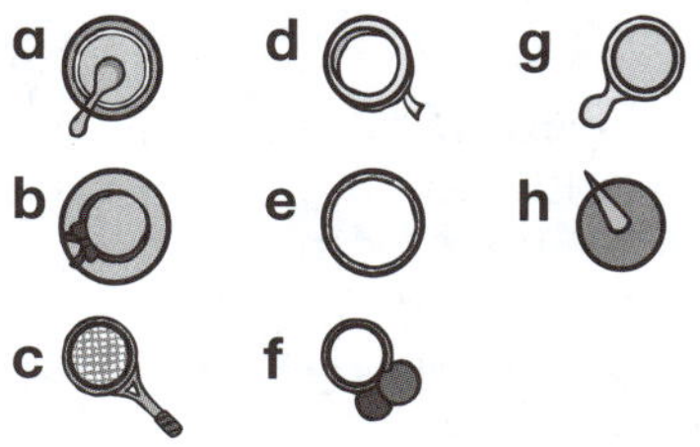

Page 4
I The pictures that should have been coloured in are:
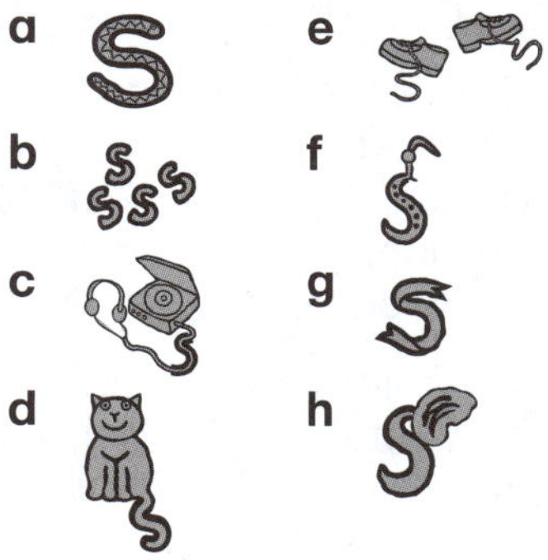

II a spoon
b sweet
c bus
d house
e shed
f seal
g past
h ask
i saw

Page 5
I

II a ink
b ring
c pink
d girl
e imp
f pig

Page 6
I
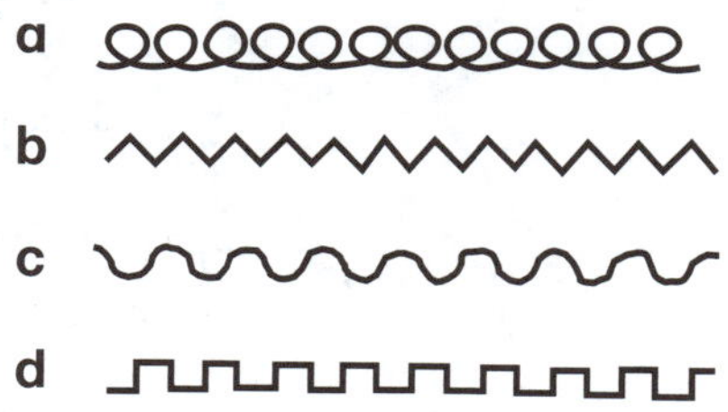

II a oooooooooooooo
b wwwwwwwwww
c ssssssssssssssssss
d cccccccccccccccc

Page 7
I a Mouse drawn under chair.
b Crown drawn on queen's head.
c Cat drawn in front of mouse.

II a Spider drawn under table.
b Bee drawn on flower.

Page 8
I a 2, 1
b 1, 2
c 1, 2
d 2, 1
e 2, 1

II a 4
b 2
c 3
d 1

Page 9
I
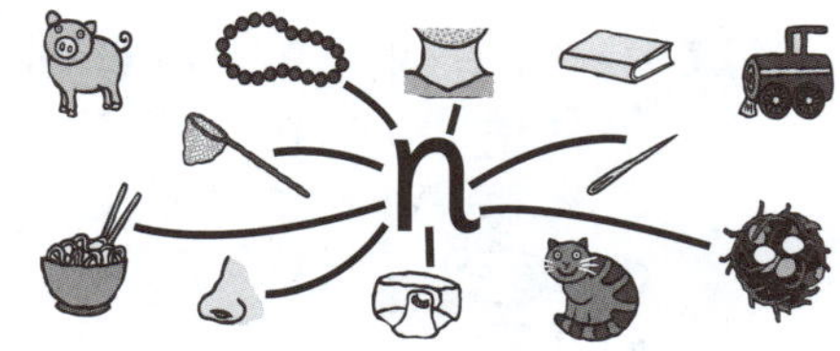

II Make sure the pictures stuck on the book shape all start with 'n'.

Page 10
I Circled words are:
a sea
b salt
c snake
d sausage
e sandwich
f silly
g sand
h starfish
i sun
j sink

II a, b, d, f, i, k

Page 11
I

II Circled words are:
a man
b pan
c ban
d mat
e sat
f bat
g fan
h dad
i rat
j lap
k pat
l ran

Page 12
I a Drawing of a windy day.
b Drawing of a snowy day.

II Check child's drawing and story.

Page 13
I
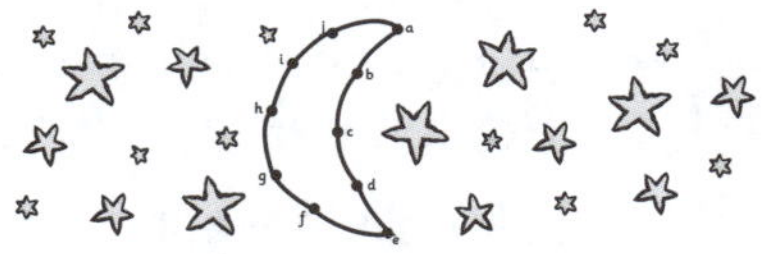

The picture is of the moon.

II a c
b f
c i
d l
e o
f r
g u
h x
i z

Page 14
I a c
b d
c r
d f
e l
f s
g m
h z

II a t
b b
c d
d h
e r
f l

Page 15
I Check child's drawing.

II Check child's writing.

Page 16

I 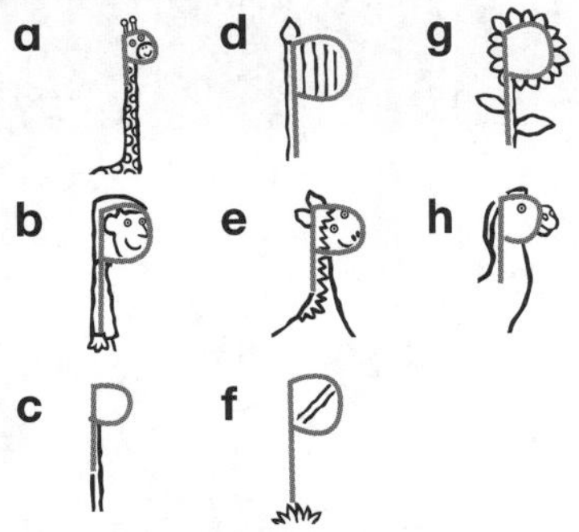

II Circled words are:

a	part	d	pot
b	past	e	pop
c	pit	f	pea

Page 17

I letters missing:
a, d, g, i, l, n, q, s, v, x

II 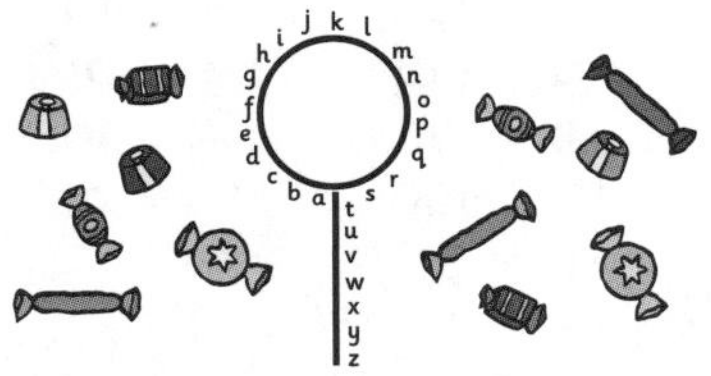

The picture is of a lolly.

Page 18

I a	October	g	March
b	January	h	April
c	December	i	February
d	November	j	July
e	August	k	May
f	September	l	June

II Check child's writing.

Page 19

I ticked: a, d, f, g

II tiger, teddy, table, tap, telephone, tape, tie, television, tennis racket

Page 20

I Check child's writing.

II 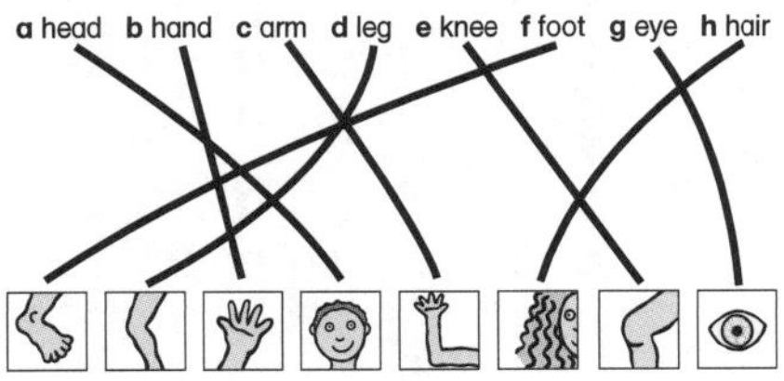

Page 21

I a	pot	e	pear
b	plate	f	pen
c	pencil	g	pig
d	pants	h	pink

II a pan
b plug, plate
c plan
d pretty, plain
e pat, pin
f play
g pen, pencil, paper
h prince

Page 22

I 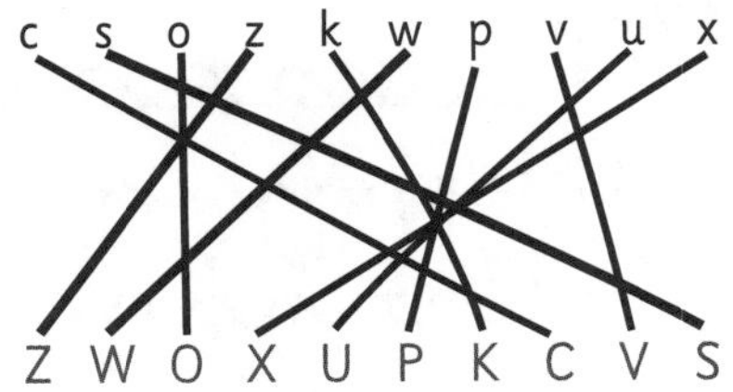

II 

Page 23

I 

II Check child's drawing.

Page 24

I a Bo Peep.
b Picture of sheep.
c Tick under picture of home.
d Picture of tails.

II a	sheep	f	wheel
b	sleep	g	peel
c	creep	h	beer
d	feet	i	beet
e	feel	j	sheet

Page 25

I Check child's writing.

II Check child's drawing.

Page 26

I 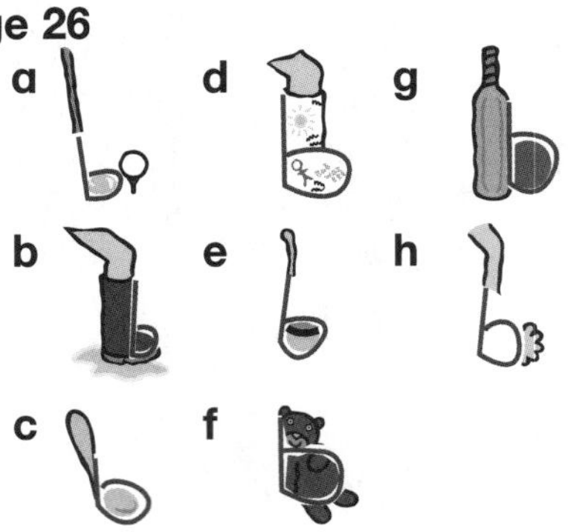

II Check child has coloured in:

a	ball	d	bin
b	book	e	bag
c	boat		

Page 27

I a Picture of a water spout.
b Picture of rain.

II Check child has coloured in: spider, spray, speak, sport, spoke.

Page 28

I Circled words are:

a	ice	f	ill
b	ink	g	into
c	I	h	in
d	idea	i	inch
e	if	j	inside

II Check child has coloured in:
a ice cream
b island
c ice skates
d igloo
e iron
f icicle

Page 29

I Check the child has coloured in:

a	nail	d	necklace
b	nappy	e	nose
c	needle	f	nest

II The following words should be written on the net:
nib, nice, no, nip, not, new, newt, nap, name.

Page 30

I Check child's colouring.

II Check child's writing.

Page 31

I 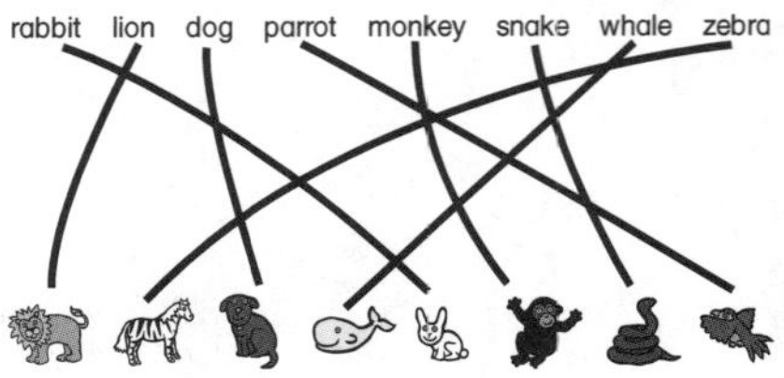

II Check child's drawing.

The letter *s*

The letter *s* looks like a snake.

It makes the **s**ame **s**ound a**s** a **s**nake. **Sssssssssssssssss sssss!**

I Circle the things that start with *s*.

a

b

c

d

II Write *s* in each space. Then draw a picture of each thing.

a ____nake

b ____oap

c ____wing

Looking at *a*

a is the first letter of the alphabet. It is in lots of words.

Can you write the letter *a*? This picture shows where to start and which way to move your pencil.

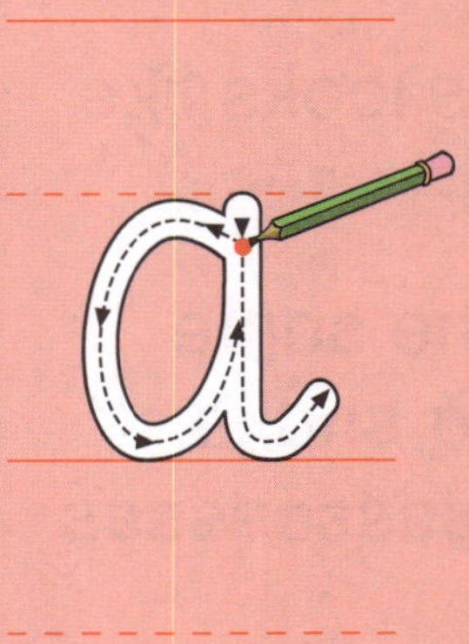

apple

baby

I Colour the pictures in each set that start with *a*.

a

apple

orange

b

leaf

acorn

c

ant

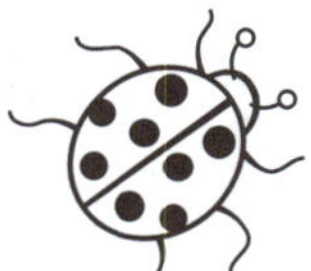

ladybird

d

alligator

cat

II Write an *a* on each apple.

Finding *i*

The letter *i* is in lots of words.

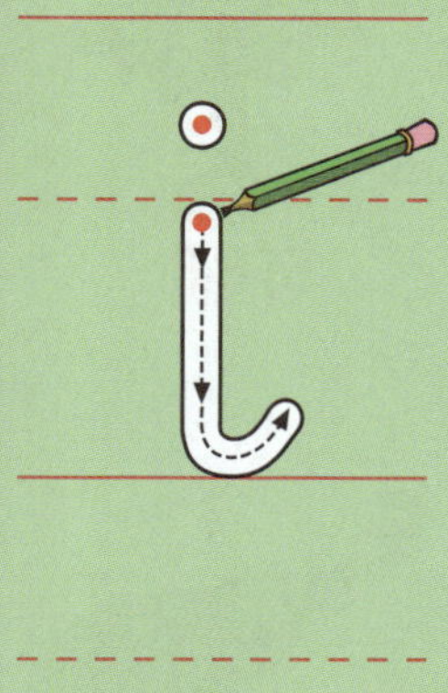

At the beginning:

igloo 

iron 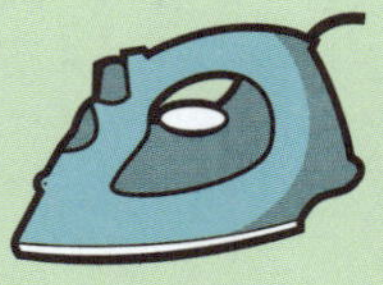

In the middle:

finish 

fish 

I Circle the words that start with *i*.

a ink pencil book

b lolly ice cream sweets

c country sea island

d pan iron cup

e flower ivy grass

f in out up

g think idea try

h ill well sick

i warm hot icy

j scratch itch stroke

II Write an *i* in these words.

a 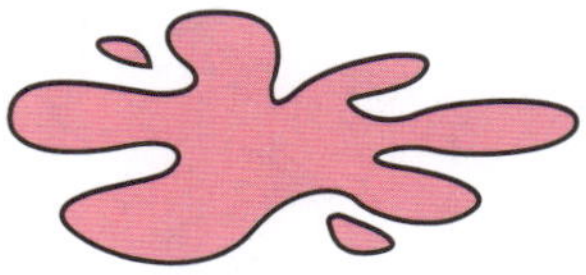

p_i_nk

c 

m_i_lk

e 

st_i_nk

b 

b_i_n

d 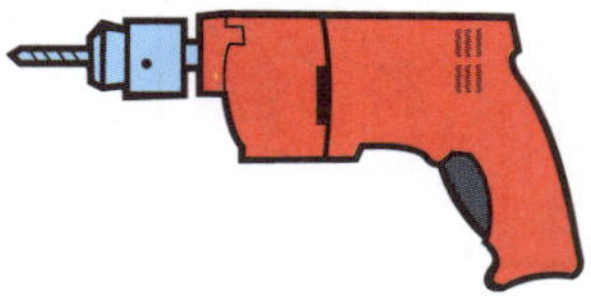

dr_i_ll

f 

_i_dea

The letter *t*

The letter *t* looks like a cross.

Can you write the letter *t*? This picture shows where to start and which way to move your pencil.

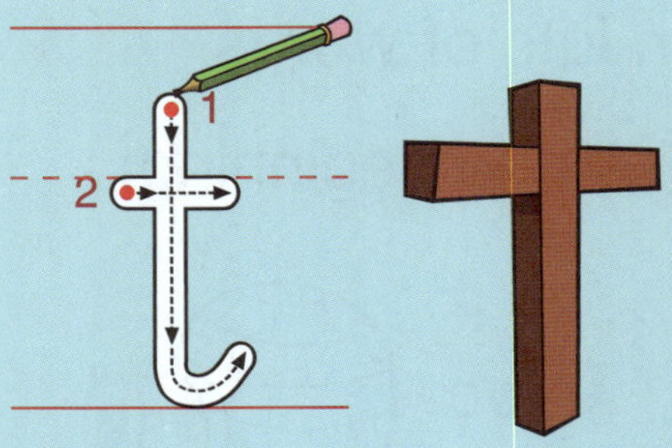

tree

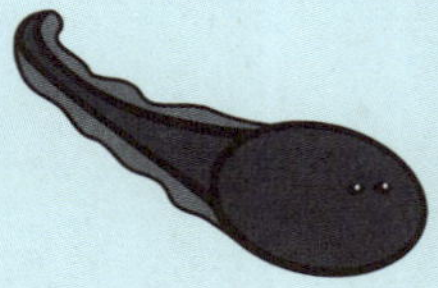

tadpole

I Circle the things that start with *t*.

a

car

b

tiger

c

television

d

chair

train

elephant

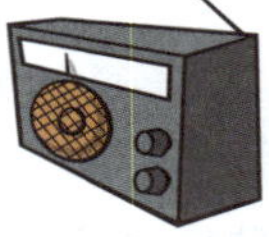

radio

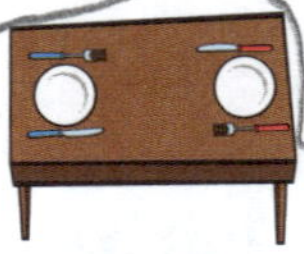

table

II Write a *t* carefully on each train carriage.

Where is *p*?

The letter *p* is made by joining a circle to a tail.

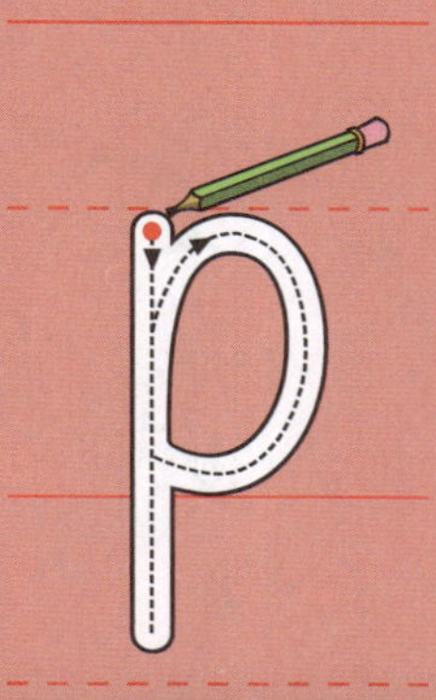

I Circle the words that start with *p*.

a draw play dance

b pool chair cream

c red green pink

d pipe soap water

e dish pan plate

f post letter card

g hand paw foot

h pen ink ruler

i rubber dice pencil

j book plants comic

II Now add the *p* to finish each word. Look at the big *p* at the top of the page to help you.

a ____ink

b ____at

c hel____

d ____ut

e co____y

f ____ull

g s ____ell

h ____itch

i ____ot

j ____it

Let's find *n*!

This picture shows where to start and which way to move your pencil to write the letter *n*.

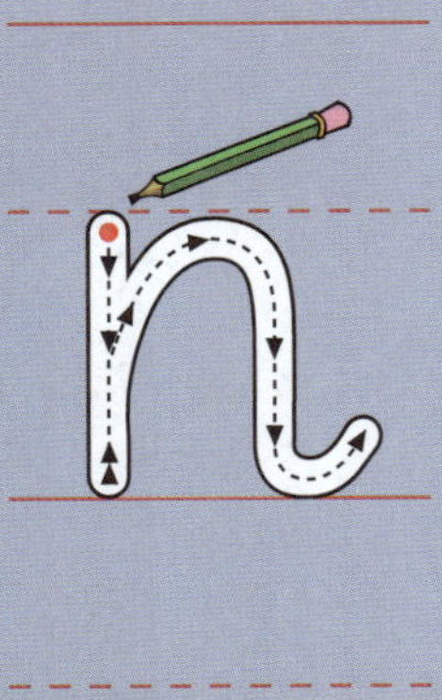

nanna

I Draw a line to join the *n* word to the picture.

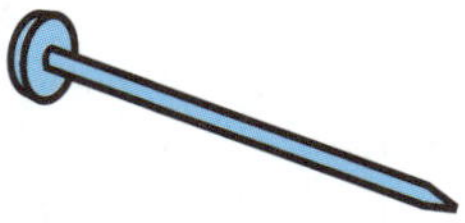

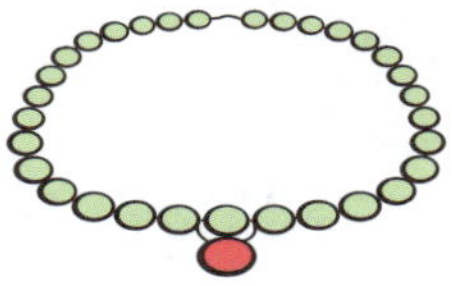

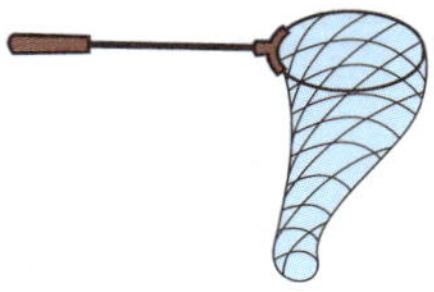

a nurse
b necklace
c nap
d nest
e nail
f net
g needle
h nut

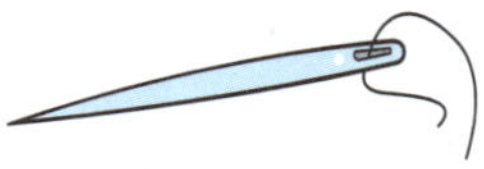

II Write an *n* on each bead of the necklace.

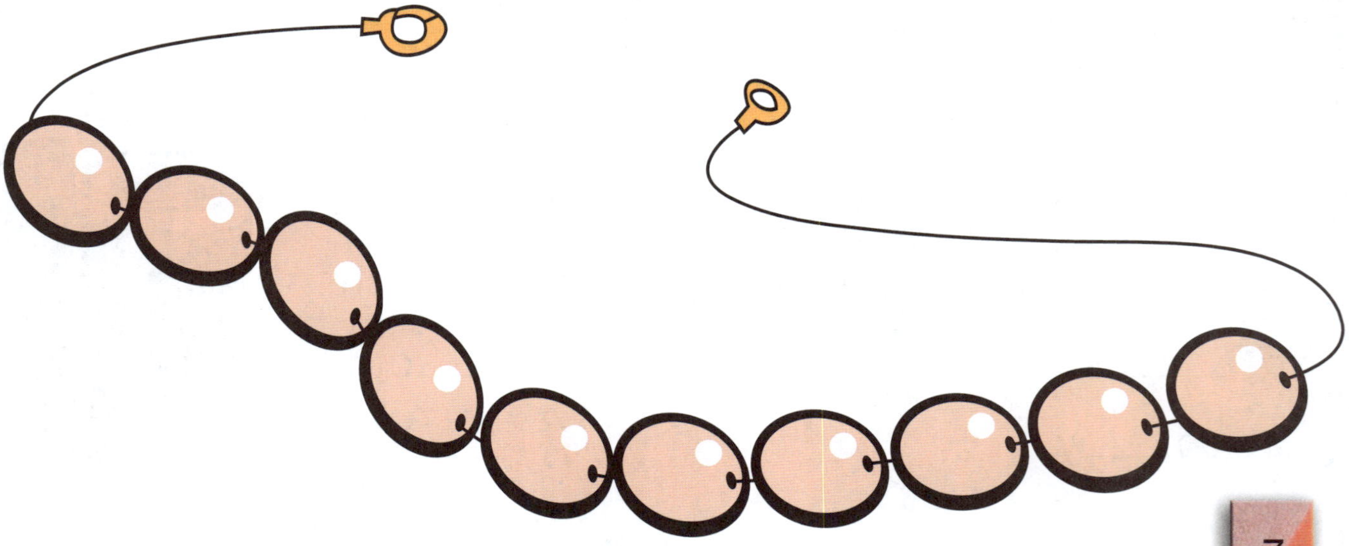

Writing *e*

This picture shows where to start and which way to move your pencil to write the letter *e*.

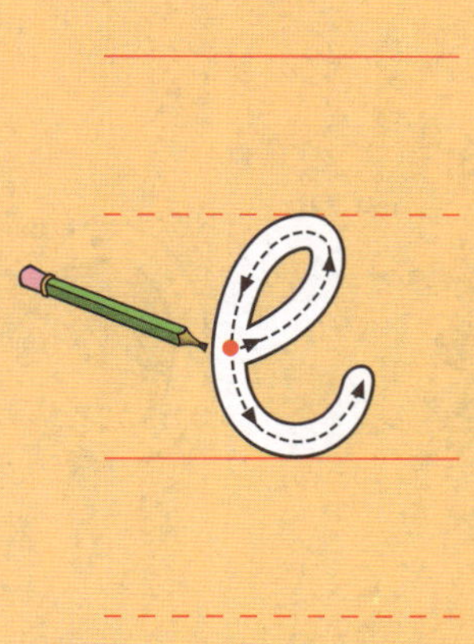

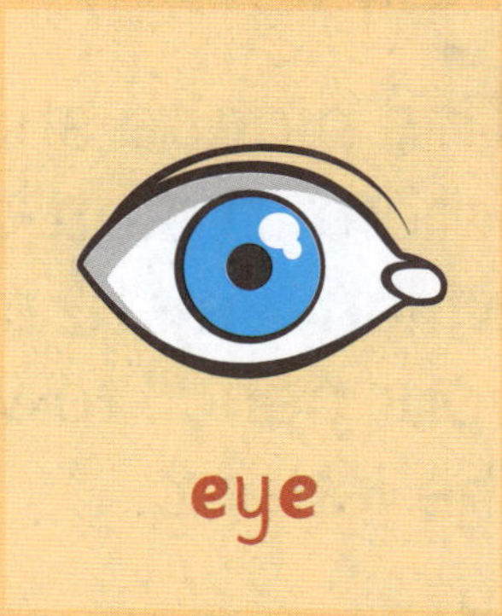

I **Colour the buns for the elephant to eat. She only likes words that start with *e*! Write the words you find below.**

a ____________________

b ____________________

c ____________________

d ____________________

e ____________________

f ____________________

II **Write an *e* on each egg.**

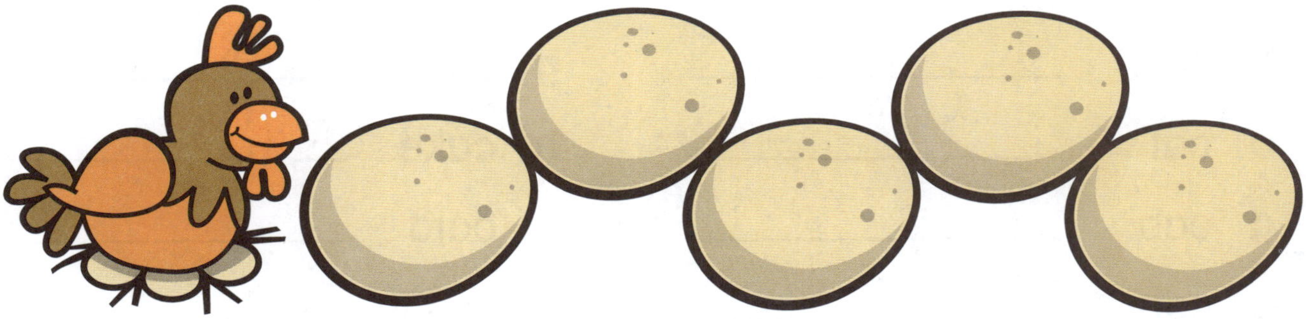

Finding *c*

This picture shows where to start and which way to move your pencil to write the letter *c*.

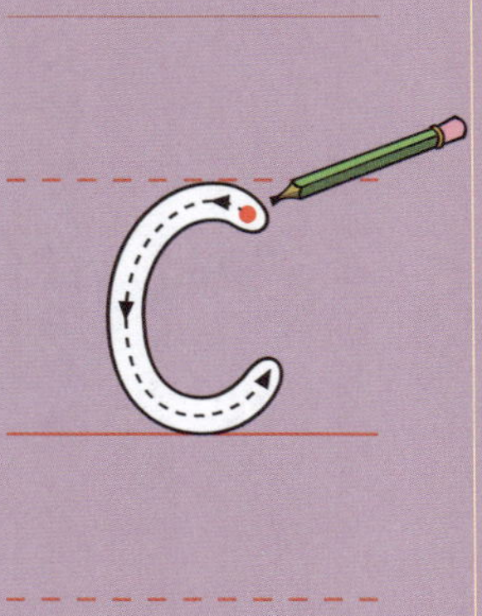

cat

cup

I Draw the things listed below in the cat shape.

a cat

b caterpillar

c cap

d car

e carrot

f cup

g coat

II Copy these words. Use your best handwriting!

a can ____________________

b car ____________________

c cat ____________________

d cab ____________________

e cap ____________________

f call ____________________

g carry ____________________

h cake ____________________

i card ____________________

j castle ____________________

The letter *u*

This picture shows where to start and which way to move your pencil to write the letter *u*.

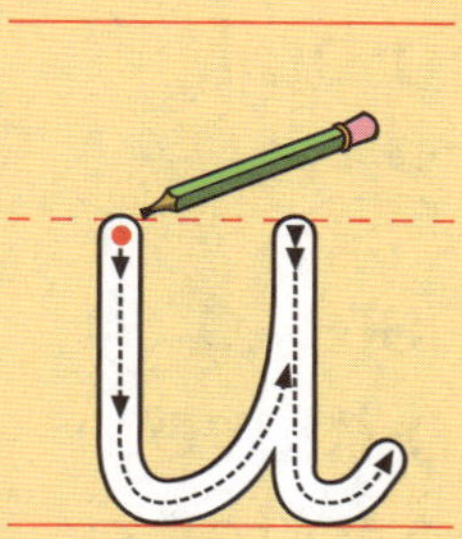

umbrella

uniform

I Colour in the raindrops that show *u* words. Then write them out.

ugly	above	all	able	us
act	and	up	under	uncle

a ______

b ______

c ______

d ______

e ______

II Copy the words onto the umbrellas.

unload

unlucky

unlock

untie

The letter *o*

The letter *o* looks like a ball.
It is a circle shape.

This picture shows where to start and which way to move your pencil to write the letter *o*.

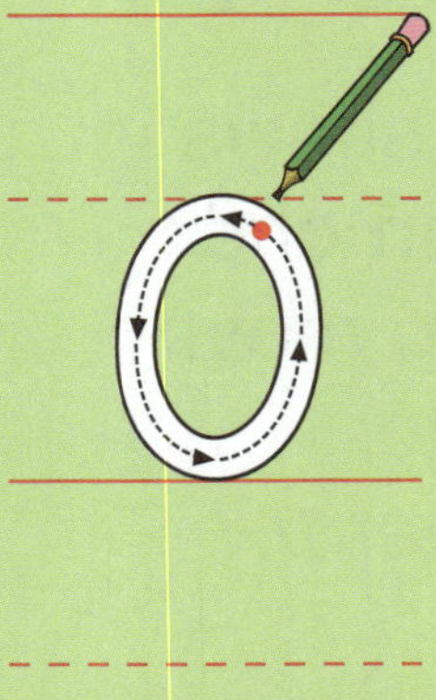

orange

I Look for the *o* words on the owl. Write them on the mice.

a

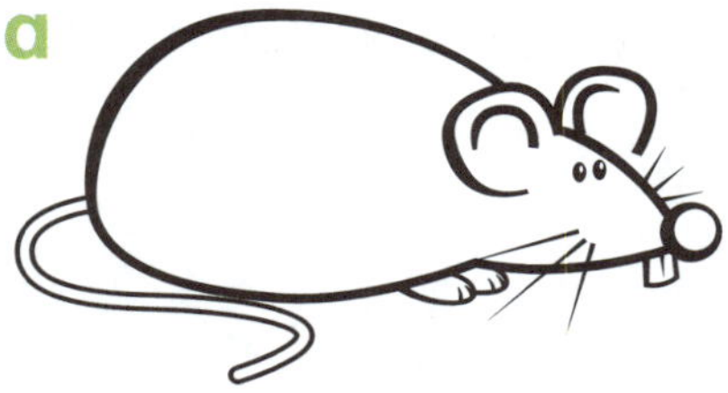

b

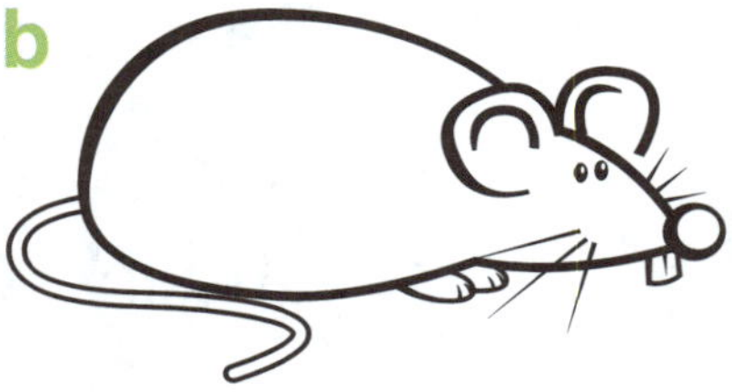

c

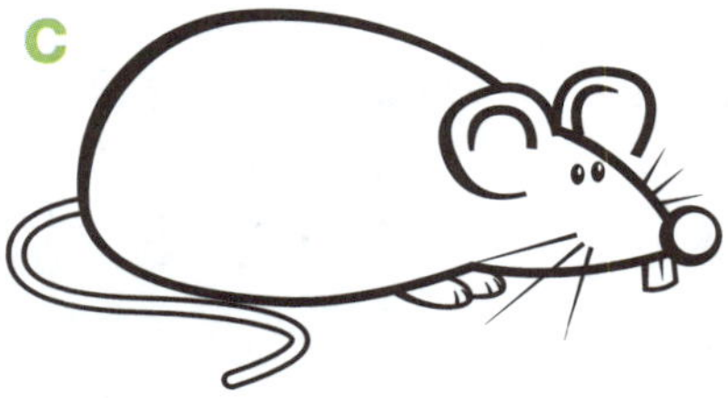

d

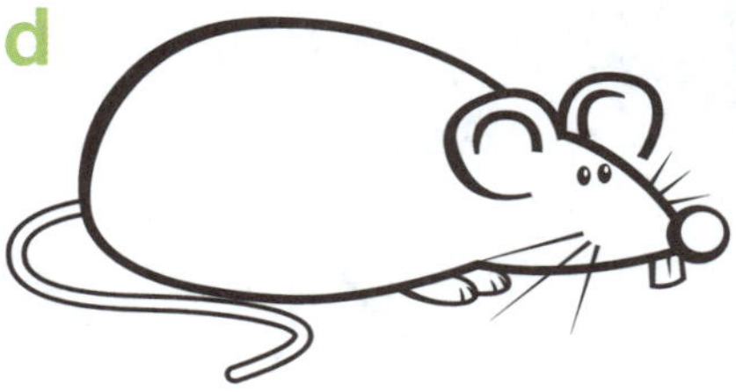

e

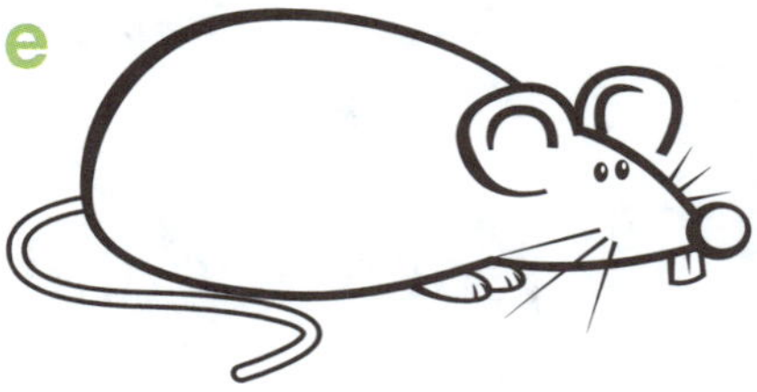

f

II Fill in the *o* to finish these words.

a s____ld

b sp____t

c c____ld

d w____rld

e m____ney

f p____p

g b____x

h w____rk

i b____w

Looking at *m*

This picture shows where to start and which way to move your pencil to write the letter *m*.

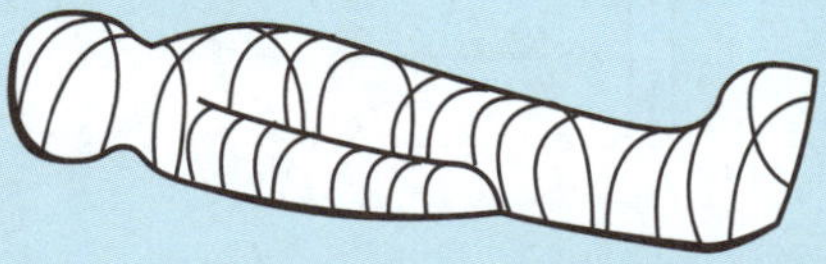

mummy

I Circle the five words beginning with *m*. Write the words below.

a ______________

b ______________

c ______________

d ______________

e ______________

II Draw 6 things that start with *m* in the boxes below.

a

b

c

d

e

f

Where is *r*?

This picture shows where to start and which way to move your pencil to write the letter *r*.

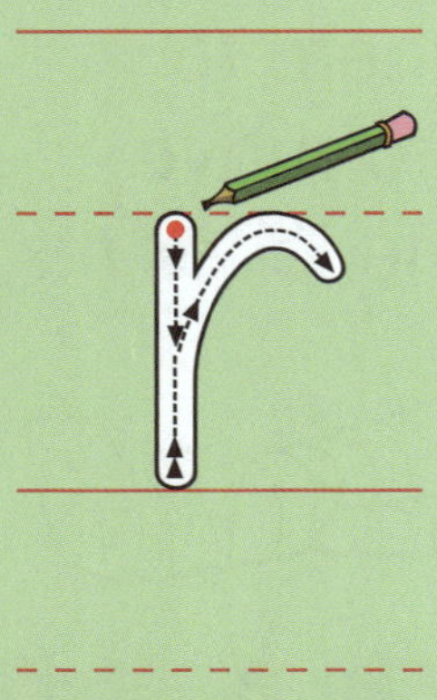

rabbit

robin

I Circle the word in each set beginning with *r*.

a	rain	snow	wind
b	string	chain	rope
c	green	yellow	red
d	rabbit	horse	duck
e	pasta	rice	soup
f	walk	crawl	run

II Draw six things beginning with *r*.

a

b

c

d

e

f

Finding *k*

k is sometimes called 'kicking k' because it looks as though there are two legs kicking out at the front!

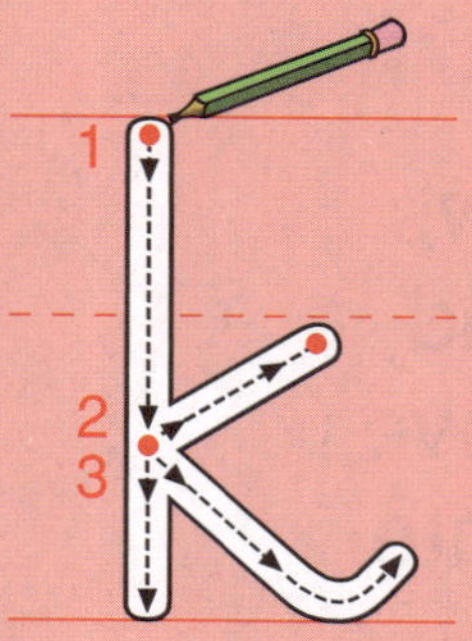

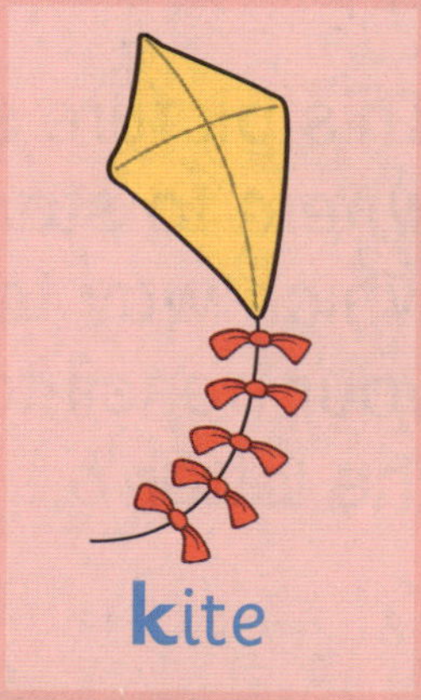

I **Draw a line from the words that start with *k* to the kangaroo. Then write the words you find in the spaces below.**

kiss kit key stamp bed

leg kind jump kettle kite

a ______________ c ______________ e ______________

b ______________ d ______________ f ______________

II **Write a *k* in these words. Draw a picture for each word.**

a cloc___ b ___itten c ___ettle

Let's find *b*!

This picture shows where to start and which way to move your pencil to write the letter *b*.

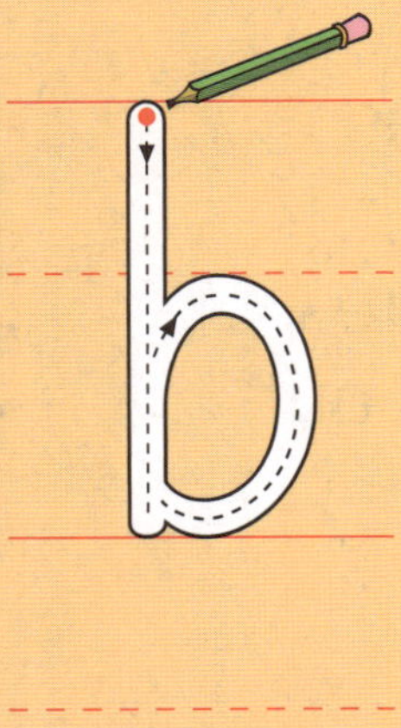

balloon

I Copy all the words that begin with *b* inside the balloon shape.

a kid, child, boy

b bad, good, nice

c kite, bat, game

d bus, car, train

e ant, bug, fly

II Write the letter *b* to finish the words.

a tu____

b ____ox

c ____end

d ____ank

e ____a____y

f ____in

g ____o____

h jo____

i ____un

The letter *d*

The letter *d* looks like a back to front *b*! Lots of people get mixed up at first. Try to remember by saying to yourself '*b* has a belly' so you remember that the round bit sticks out in front on a *b*, not a *d*!

I **Draw a line to join the *d* words to the dog. Then write the words underneath.**

drum deer duck cat

hat doll

dress purse candle door

a ______________ **c** ______________ **e** ______________

b ______________ **d** ______________ **f** ______________

II **Write the letter *d* in the spaces carefully to finish the words.**

a ma___e **d** bo___y **g** car___

b she___ **e** ___rain **h** ___esk

c ___isc **f** ___oll **i** han___le

Finding l

The letter l is easy to write. It is just a line straight down with a little curl at the bottom.

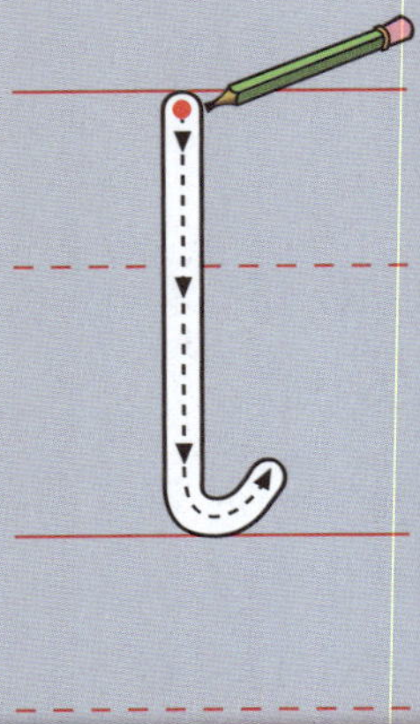

I Write an l carefully on each leaf.

II Circle the things that start with l. Tick the words as you find each thing.

- a lamp ☐
- b letter ☐
- c light ☐
- d lock ☐
- e lady ☐
- f lemon ☐
- g ladybird ☐
- h lollipop ☐
- i lorry ☐
- j lamb ☐

The letter *f*

The letter *f* is like a cross, or the letter *t*. You draw a long stick first, and then cross it with a shorter stick.

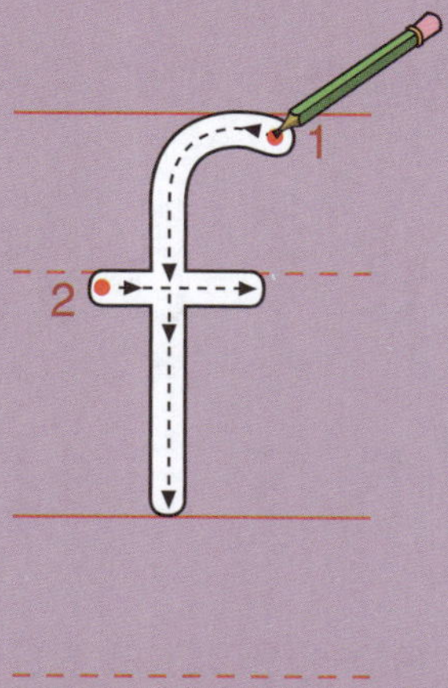

I Draw a line to join the pictures to the word.

a flag

b face

c fin

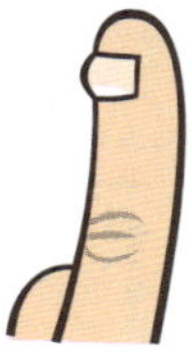

d finger

e five

f fire

II Draw something that starts with *f* on each fish shape. Then write the word.

a

____

c

____

e

____

b

____

d

____

f

____

Writing lower case letters

a b c d e f g h i j k l m

n o p q r s t u v w x y z

Write **carefully**, so people can read what you say.

I **Copy these letters across the page until the line is full. Remember to check that you are writing the letter in the correct way.**

a s ______________________________

b a ______________________________

c c ______________________________

d e ______________________________

II **Now copy these groups of letters across the page until the line is full. Do you recognise all of the letters?**

a bpbp ______________________________

b fgfg ______________________________

c pqpq ______________________________

d zzzz ______________________________

Writing capital letters

A B C D E F G H I J K L M

N O P Q R S T U V W X Y Z

Capital letters are the letters we use at the beginning of a sentence, and for the names of people and places.

My name is **S**am. **I** live in **L**ondon.

I **Copy the capital letters across the page until the line is full. These letters are made up from straight lines, so they are not too hard!**

a A ____

b E ____

c K ____

d T ____

II **Now try these. These capitals have some curves or rounded parts. Copy the letters across the page until the line is full.**

a O ____

b Q ____

c S ____

Letter blend *ch*

When we add the letters *c* and *h* together, we make a new sound *ch*.
More than one letter put together to make a sound is called a **blend**.

c + at = **c**at

h + at = **h**at

ch + at = **ch**at

I Write the *ch* words you find on the chest on the lump of cheese.

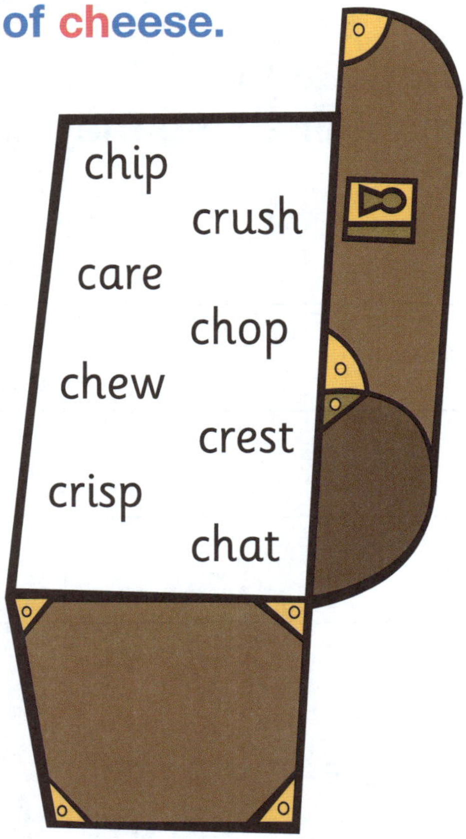

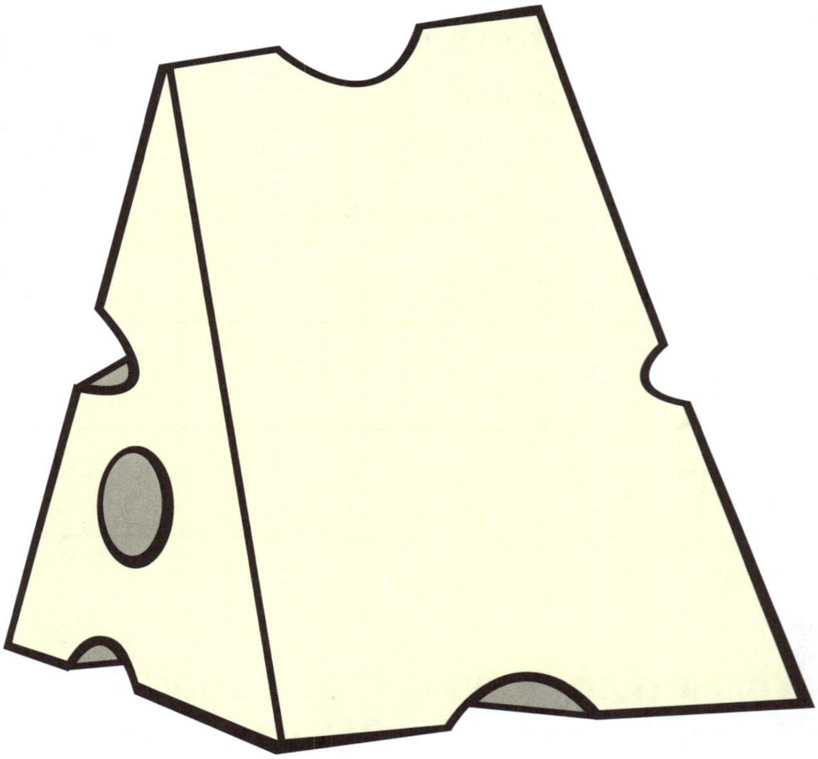

II Write *ch* to finish the words.

a ____art

b mu____

c swit____

d ____imp

e snat____

f crun____

g ____in

h lat____

i ____at

Letter blend *sh*

When we add the letters *s* and *h* together, we make a new sound *sh*. More than one letter put together to make a sound is called a **blend**.

s + h = sh

I Join the *sh* words to the ship with a wavy line. Then write them below.

shriek

space

spoon

ship

shin

shall

small

shave

shine

a ______________ c ______________ e ______________

b ______________ d ______________ f ______________

II Write *sh* to finish the words.

a _____arp

b _____ade

c sma_____

d thra_____

e tra_____

f _____ark

g _____in

h wa_____

i _____op

j wi_____

Letter blend *th*

When we add the letters *t* and *h* together, we make a new sound *th*. We have made a **blend**.

t + h = th

When we make the sound *th*, we put our tongue between our teeth and blow. Try it!

I Write *th* to finish the words.

a ______ump
b ______em
c ______ick
d ______ink
e ______en
f ______at
g ______is
h ______ese
i ______ose

II Choose a *th* word from the box to finish each sentence.

thump	the	then	this	think	these	thank	thick

a '______________ you!' said Julie.
b What is ______________ time?
c ______________ are my favourites!
d What is ______________?
e ______________ I came home.
f I fell down with a ______________.
g My milkshake is really ______________.
h I ______________ I would like a cheese sandwich.

Rhymes

Do you like poems with words that rhyme? We say words rhyme when they make the same sound.

The **cat** **sat** on the m**at** looking at a b**at**.

Cat, **sat**, m**at** and b**at** all rhyme because they all use the sound *at*.

I Circle the word that rhymes with the word in the picture.

a cat  bat fish dog

b book  read look write

c door  carpet table floor

d wear  rip tear use

e hop  pop jump pip

II Match the words so they all rhyme with their partner.

a had b nut c did d red e ball f key g pay h hot

tall hid cut me bad day not bed

Same sounds

Poems often have lots of words that start with the same sound. If someone wanted to write a poem about snakes, they might write about **sn**eaky **sn**akes, because both words start with the same sound – and it makes it sound as though there is a slithery snake about!

I Draw a line from each word to the word that starts with the same sound.

a smelly b tiny c green d red e big f lovely g dirty

lady dog grass bunny robin skunk toes

II Draw pictures of things that start with the same sound as the words.

a pink

c kind

e cold

b shiny

d funny

f big

Book language

When you talk about books, you need to be able to use 'book language'. There are special words to describe different things that you find in or on books.

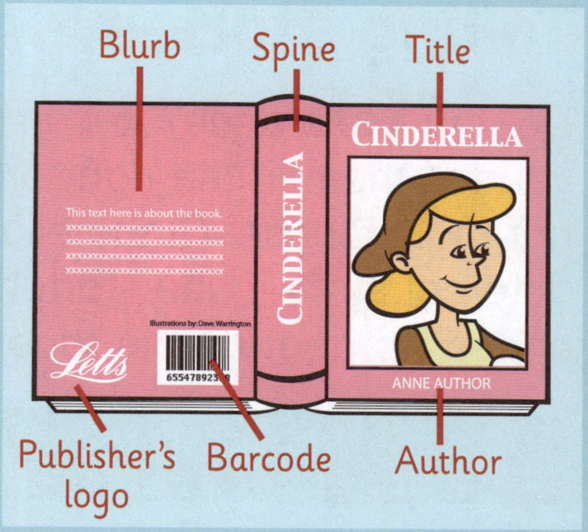

I Draw a line from each word to its book part.

a title	The name of the person who wrote the book.
b author	The name of the person who drew the pictures.
c illustrator	The name of the book.
d spine	Information about the book to make you want to buy it.
e blurb	The part of the book that joins the front cover and the back cover.

II Draw your own book cover. Include the things in the box.

title
publisher's logo
spine
blurb
front cover picture

Telling stories

Do you like stories? It is important that you tell them in the right order, or they do not make sense. Cinderella would be a different story if she started off rich and ended up poor and in rags!

I **Read the sentences below and put them in the correct order to tell the story.**

a Then they all lived happily ever after. ____

b So they chased him away with buckets of soapy water. ____

c Once upon a time, there were three little wolves who lived with their mum. ____

d The wolves knew that the pig hated to be clean. ____

e One day, a scary pig came to steal fruit from their garden. ____

II **Now draw your own story by drawing pictures in the boxes below. It can be about anything you like – fairies, football, animals, space – you choose! Just make sure it is in the right order, so it makes sense.**

a

b

c

op words

You see the letters *op* in lots of words.

pop 

shop 

I Add *op* to make a word.

a t_____

b p_____

c h_____

d c_____

e b_____

f m_____

g l_____

h dr_____

i cr_____

II Draw a line from each word to its picture.

top

pop

hop

cop

bop

mop

crop

drop

flop

plop

an words

Lots of words use the letters *a* and *n* together.

man  fan 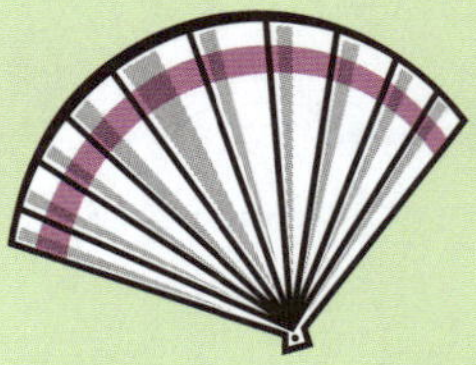

I Add *an* to make a word.

a r_____

b t_____

c p_____

d f_____

e c_____

f b_____

g m_____

h h_____d

i b_____d

j w_____d

II Draw a line from each word to its picture.

ran		man
pan		wand
fan		band
hand		orange
can		tan

at words

Lots of words end in the letter blend *at*.

hat

bat

cat

I Add *at* to make a word.

a r_____

b spl_____

c p_____

d s_____

e f_____

f h_____

g c_____

h b_____

i m_____

j br_____

II Draw a line from each word to its picture.

rat

pat

sat

fat

hat

cat

bat

mat

chat

bat

ip words

You will see the letters *ip* in lots of words.

drip

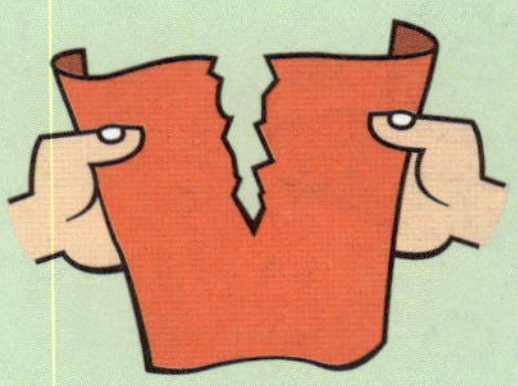
rip

I Add *ip* to make a word.

a r_____
b t_____
c p_____
d s_____
e d_____
f h_____
g l_____
h n_____
i dr_____
j sl_____

II Circle the words that end in *ip*.

a rip rap roll
b top toll tip
c pop pull pip
d sat sip sap
e dog dip dig
f hop hall hip
g lip lap lot
h nip nap not

ANSWERS

Page 2

I Circled:
a sheep **b** scarf **c** swan **d** shirt

II **a** snake **b** soap **c** swing

Page 3

I Coloured:
a apple **b** acorn **c** ant **d** alligator

II 'a' written on all the apples

Page 4

I Circled:
a ink **b** ice cream **c** island **d** iron **e** ivy **f** in **g** idea **h** ill **i** icy **j** itch

II **a** pink **b** bin **c** milk **d** drill **e** stink **f** idea

Page 5

I Circled:
a train **b** tiger **c** television **d** table

II 't' written in train carriages

Page 6

I Circled:
a play **b** pool **c** pink **d** pipe **e** pan, plate **f** post **g** paw **h** pen **i** pencil **j** plants

II **a** pink **b** pat **c** help **d** put **e** copy **f** pull **g** spell **h** pitch **i** pot **j** pit

Page 7

I

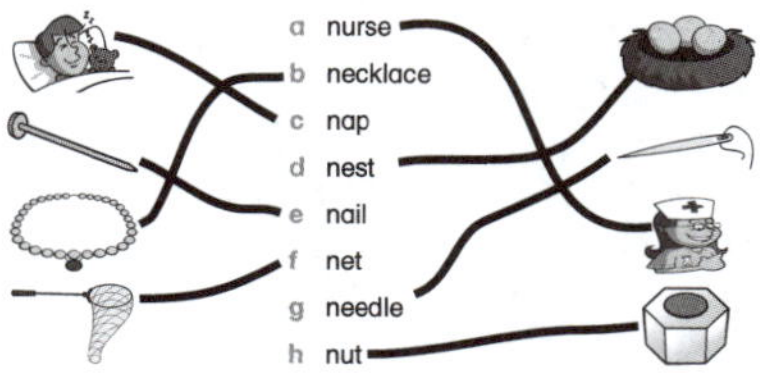

II 'n' written on each bead

Page 8

I Coloured and words written in any order:
a egg **b** earth **c** eight **d** ear **e** eat **f** eel

II 'e' written on each egg

Page 9

I Pictures drawn as asked.

II Words copied correctly.

Page 10

I Words written in any order:
a ugly **b** up **c** under **d** uncle **e** us

II Words written in any order on umbrellas.

Page 11

I Words copied onto mice in any order:
a out **b** odd **c** old **d** our **e** oar **f** ocean

II **a** sold **b** spot **c** cold **d** world **e** money **f** pop **g** box **h** work **i** bow

Page 12

I Circled: medal, monkey, map, mud, mouse. Words written in any order.

II 6 things starting with the letter *m*.

Page 13

I **a** rain **b** rope **c** red **d** rabbit **e** rice **f** run

II 6 things beginning with *r*.

Page 14

I Joined (then written in any order):
a kiss **b** key **c** kettle **d** kit **e** kind **f** kite

II **a** clock **b** kitten **c** kettle
Pictures of the above drawn in the spaces.

Page 15

I **a** boy **b** bad **c** bat **d** bus **e** bug

II **a** tub **b** box **c** bend **d** bank **e** baby **f** bin **g** bob **h** job **i** bun

Page 16

I Joined (and the words then written in any order):
a drum **b** dress **c** deer **d** duck **e** doll **f** door

II **a** made **b** shed **c** disc **d** body **e** drain **f** doll **g** card **h** desk **i** handle

Page 17

I *l* written on each leaf.

II Items ticked as child shows them to an adult.

Page 18

I

II Anything that starts with the letter *f*, drawn on the shapes and then written, i.e. fox, finger, face.

Page 19

I Letters written carefully and correctly formed across the page.

II Letters written carefully and correctly formed across the page.

Page 20

I Letters written carefully and correctly formed across the page.

II Letters written carefully and correctly formed across the page.

Page 21

I Copied: chop, chew, chip, chat.

II **a** chart **b** much **c** switch **d** chimp **e** snatch **f** crunch **g** chin **h** latch **i** chat

Page 22

I Joined (then written in any order):
a shriek **b** ship **c** shin **d** shall **e** shave **f** shine

II **a** sharp **b** shade **c** smash **d** thrash **e** trash **f** shark **g** shin **h** wash **i** shop **j** wish

Page 23

I **a** thump **b** them **c** thick **d** think **e** then **f** that **g** this **h** these **i** those

II **a** thank **b** the **c** these **d** this **e** then **f** thump **g** thick **h** think

Page 24

I **a** bat **b** look **c** floor **d** tear **e** pop

II **a** bad **b** cut **c** hid **d** bed **e** tall **f** me **g** day **h** not

Page 25

I **a** skunk **b** toes **c** grass **d** robin **e** bunny **f** lady **g** dog

II Any suitable drawings; for example: 'kind' could be kangaroo.

Page 26

I **a** The name of the book.
b The name of the person who wrote the book.
c The name of the person who drew the pictures.
d The part of the book that joins the front cover and the back cover.
e Information about the book to make you want to buy it.

II Book cover coloured in, containing all the elements listed.

Page 27

I **a** 5 **b** 4 **c** 1 **d** 3 **e** 2

II 3 pictures to tell a story – ask your child to tell the story.

Page 28

I **a** top **b** pop **c** hop **d** cop **e** bop **f** mop **g** lop **h** drop **i** crop

II
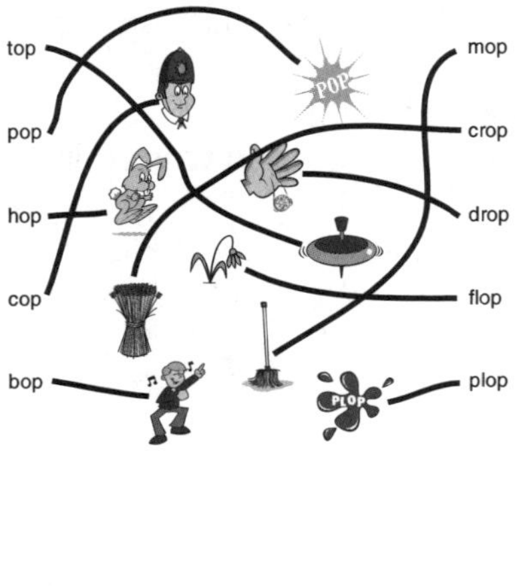

Page 29

I **a** ran **b** tan **c** pan **d** fan **e** can **f** ban **g** man **h** hand **i** band **j** wand

II
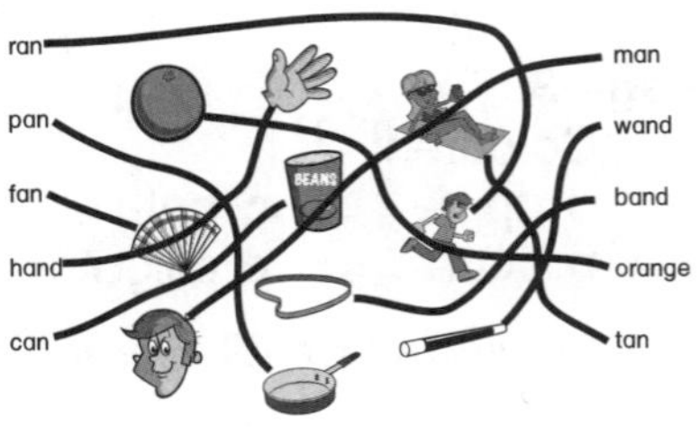

Page 30

I **a** rat **b** splat **c** pat **d** sat **e** fat **f** hat **g** cat **h** bat **i** mat **j** brat

II
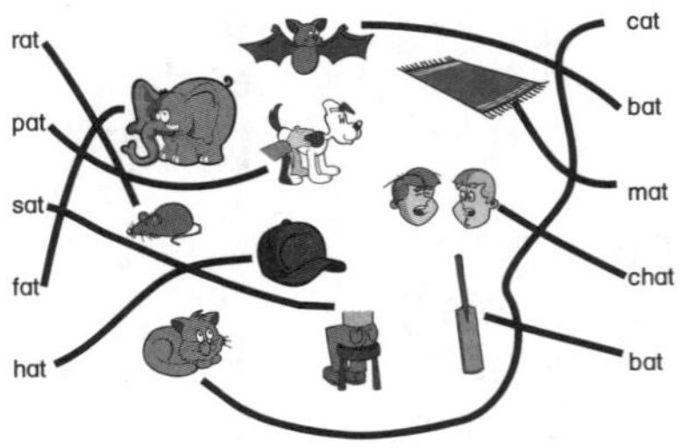

Page 31

I **a** rip **b** tip **c** pip **d** sip **e** dip **f** hip **g** lip **h** nip **i** drip **j** slip

II Circled:
a rip **b** tip **c** pip **d** sip **e** dip **f** hip **g** lip **h** nip

Make it easy...

Maths

Age 3-5

Hidden objects

Look at the **shapes** of objects to work out what they are.

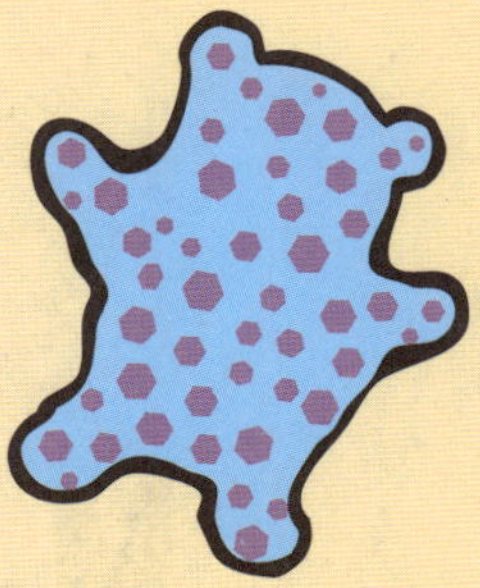

Think about what this could be.

I Can you work out which object is hidden in these 5 presents?

car doll boat kite train

a

b

c

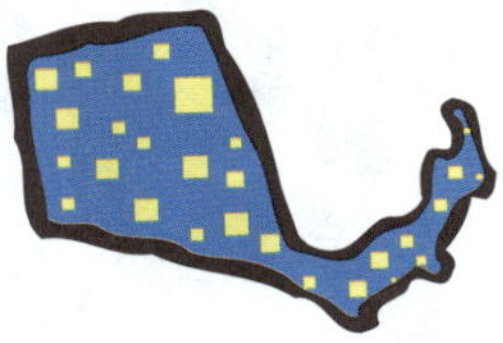

d

e

II Find five balloons hidden in this picture.

Matching pairs

A pair of objects are **two** things that go together.

I Draw lines to join the matching pairs.

II Draw patterns and colour these socks to make matching pairs.

a

b

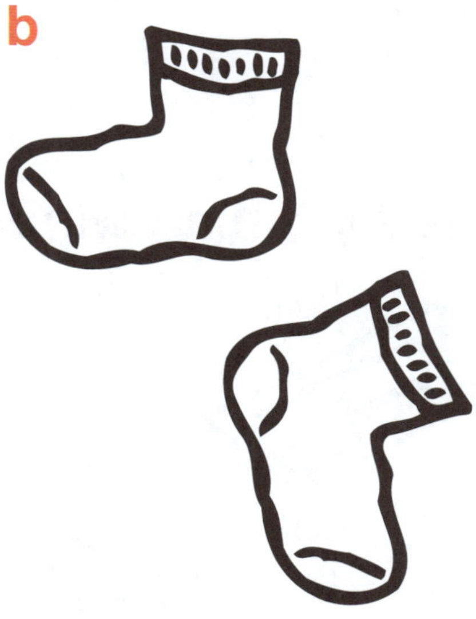

c

Matching shapes

Look at objects in **different positions**.

Talk about the **shapes**.

I Draw lines to join the matching objects.

II Colour to show the matching windows.

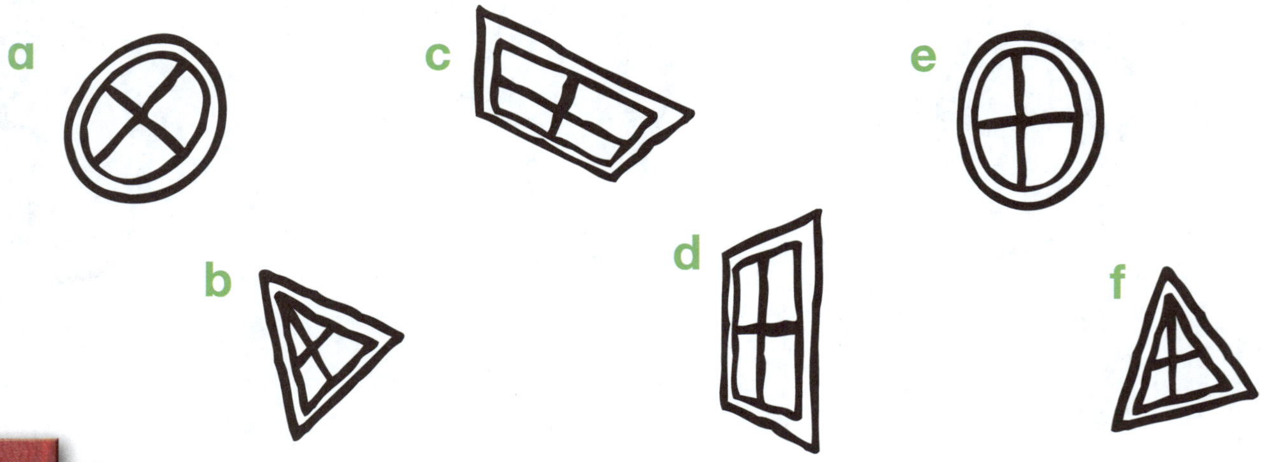

Sorting pairs

The **shapes** and **patterns** on objects can help to sort matching pairs.

I Draw lines to join the pairs that match.

II Colour to show the matching shoes.

Odd one out

The odd one out of a set could be a **different shape** or have **different colours**.

I Circle the odd one out on each plate.

a

c

b

d

II Draw a cross on the odd one out in each row.

a

b

c

Sorting

You can sort by putting things that go together into **sets**.

These bricks have been sorted into colours.

I Point to things that go together.

II Draw a line to sort the same size bricks into sets.

Spot the difference

Differences are things that are **not the same**. Look at shapes and colours to find differences.

I Put a circle around the 5 differences in these two pictures.

II Draw a pattern on the mat to make it different from the first one.

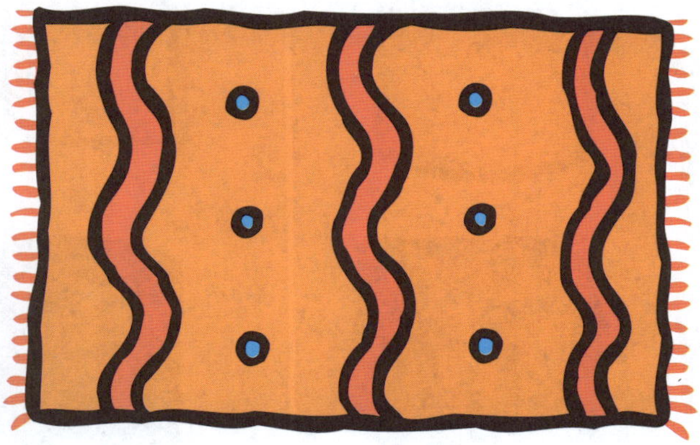

Matching colours

Do you know these colours?

I Draw a line to match each hat to its colour.

II Colour the lids to match the boxes.

Patterns

Look for patterns all around you.

I Point to each pattern in this picture.

II Draw lines to join the matching patterns.

Find the way

Find the way by using your finger to **follow** the path.

Try not to go over the edges.

I Draw a line to follow each path.

a

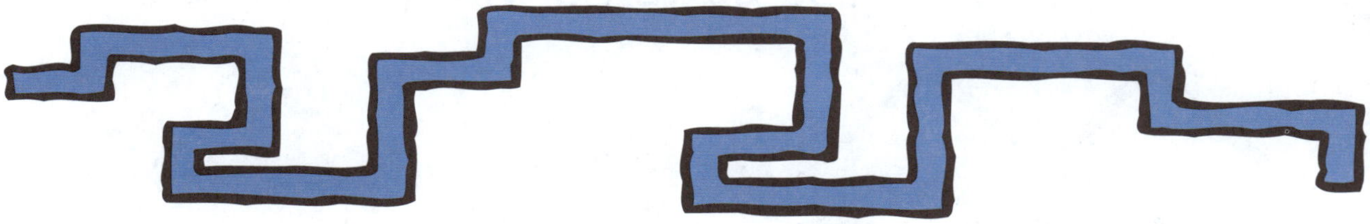

b

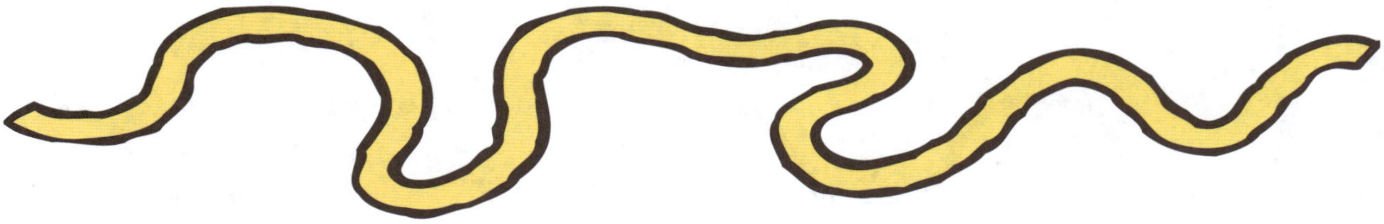

II Find your way through this maze. Go past the ball and teddy on your way.

Copying patterns

Move your hand and pencil smoothly to copy patterns.

Don't press too hard!

I Carefully finish these patterns with your pencil.

a 

b 

c 

d 

II These are a bit trickier. Try to follow them to the end.

a 

b 

c 

All about *1* and *2*

Talk about the numbers **1** and **2**.

I Draw lines to join the number of pieces of fruit in each bowl to the correct numbers.

II Draw the right number of dots on the dice.

a

b

All about *3* and *4*

Talk about the numbers **3** and **4**.

three

3 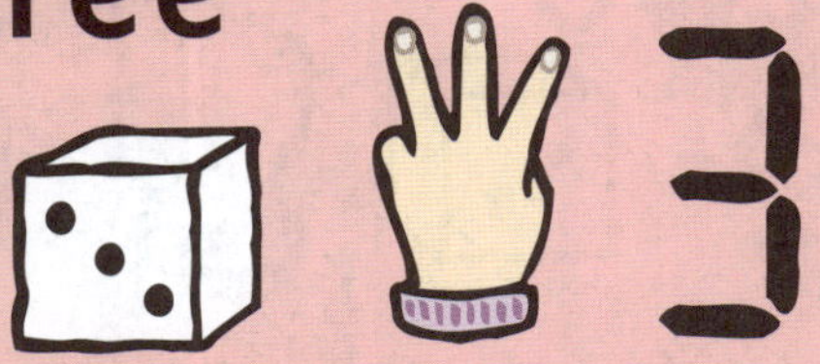

four

4 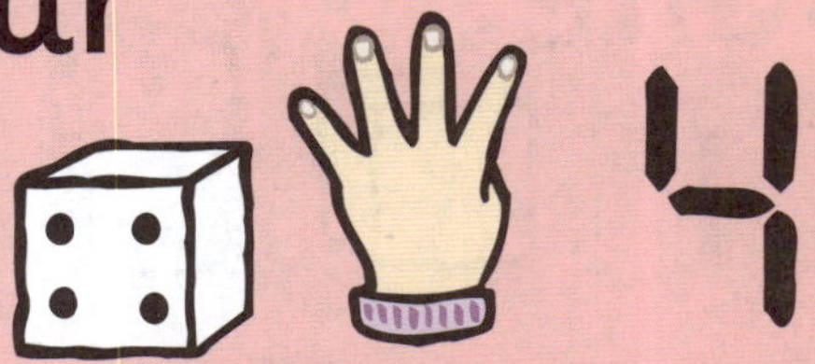

I **Colour the balls with 3 spots red. Colour the balls with 4 spots blue.**

II **Count the flags. Draw a circle round the correct number below.**

a

1	2	3	4

b

1	2	3	4

Sizes

Compare the size of things.

This is a **small** tree.

This is a **big** tree.

I Draw lines to join each squirrel to the correct size nut.

a

b

c

II Draw a small bird and a large bird to go in the correct nests.

Shapes all around us

Look at the shapes of things.

How are they **different**?

How are they the **same**?

I Draw lines to join each person to their shadow.

a

b

c

d

e

f

II Cross out the odd flower from each of these groups.

a

b

c

Comparing lengths

Compare the length of objects.

This is a **long** belt.

This is a **short** belt.

I Circle the longest snake and the shortest snake.

II Draw tails on these mice.

a Draw a long tail.

b Draw a short tail.

Recognising shapes

Look for things around you that **match** these shapes.

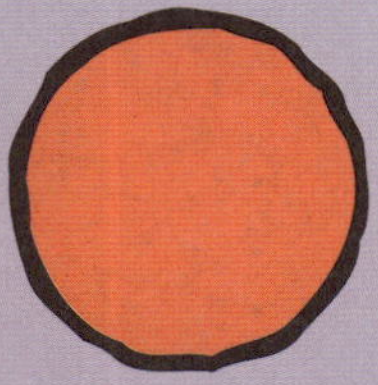

circle

square

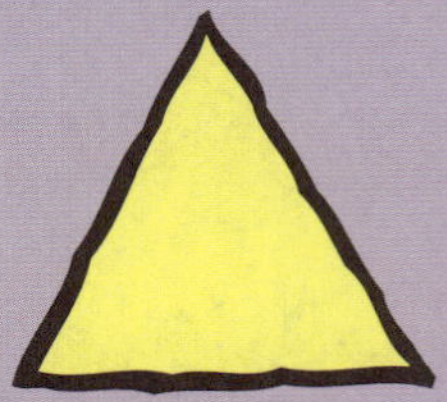

triangle

I Draw lines to join each object to its shape.

II Colour the shapes to match and finish the picture.

Numbers to *3*

Learn the shapes of the numbers **1**, **2** and **3**.

1

2

3

I Count the toys. Join each group to its matching number.

1

2

3

II Colour the odd one out in each row.

a

b

c

All about *5* and *6*

Here are the numbers **5** and **6**.

five

5 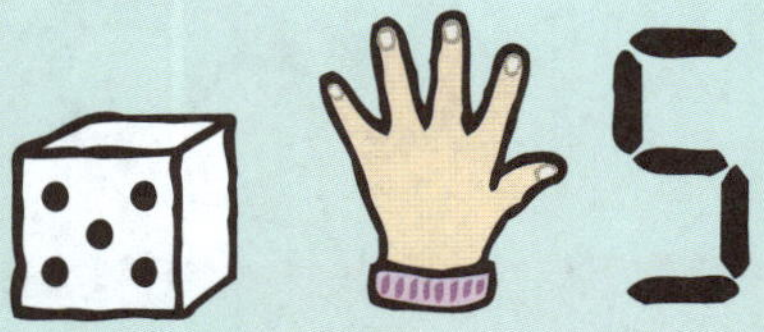

six

6 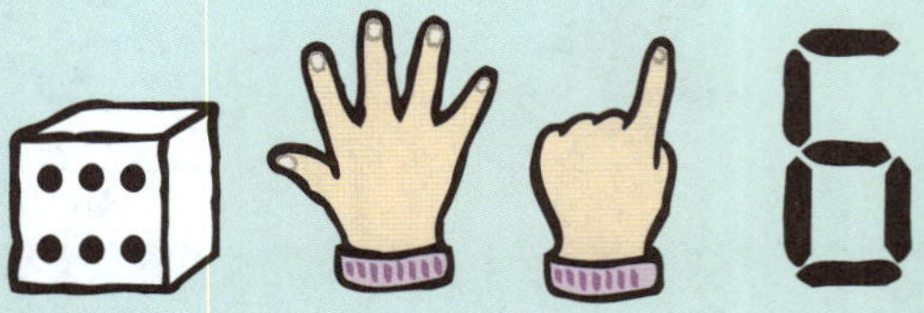

I Count the objects on each card. Draw lines to join the cards to the correct numbers.

5

6

II Draw the same number of dots below each number.

a

5 

b

6 

All about *7* and *8*

Here are the numbers **7** and **8**.

seven

7 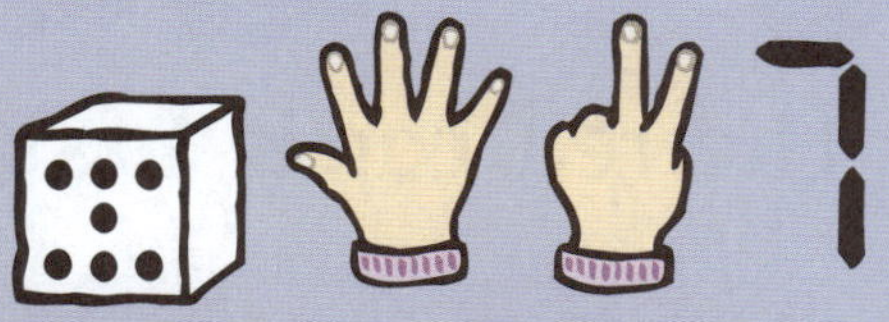

eight

8 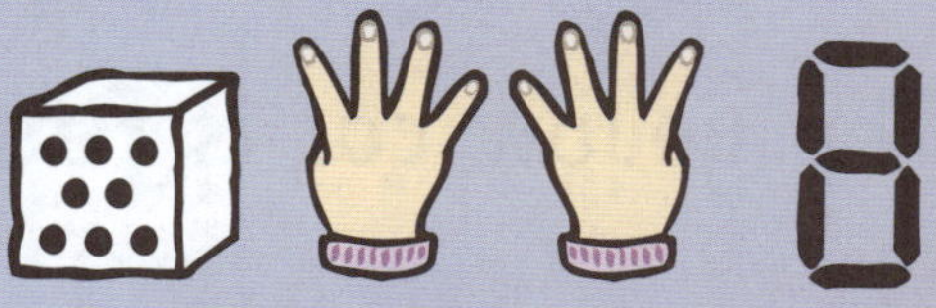

I Colour the bugs with 7 spots yellow. Colour the bugs with 8 spots green.

II Count the bugs and draw a circle round the correct number.

a

5	6	7	8

b

5	6	7	8

First and last

The yellow car is **first**. The red car is **last**.

I Colour the first in each row *blue* and colour the last in *red*.

a

b

c

II Draw a hat on the person who is first in the queue.

Draw a scarf on the person who is last in the queue.

Counting to *5*

When you count things, the **last number** tells you how many there are.

I **Count the buttons on each shirt. Draw lines to join the matching shirts.**

II **Draw dots on the balloons to match the numbers on the baskets.**

More counting

Use a **number line** to help learn the numbers.
Count these numbers out loud.

1 2 3 4 5

I **Count the apples in each tree. Join each tree to the correct number on the number line.**

1 2 3 4 5

II **Each ladybird needs 5 spots. Draw the extra spots.**

a b c d

Recognising numbers

Follow the **shapes** of these **numbers** with your finger.

I Colour each car to match the numbers below.

II Cross out the odd one on each line.

a
b
c
d

Writing numbers

Practise writing these numbers.

1 2 3 4 5

I **Draw over the numbers. Start at the red dots.**

a 1 1 1 1 1 1

b 2 2 2 2 2

c 3 3 3 3 3

d 4 4 4 4 4

e 5 5 5 5 5

II **Trace over the numbers. Draw spots to match the numbers.**

a 1

b 2

c 3

d 4

e 5

Matching numbers

These are matching dogs.

The dogs both have **4 spots**.

I Draw the same number of spots to match.

a

b

c

d

e

f

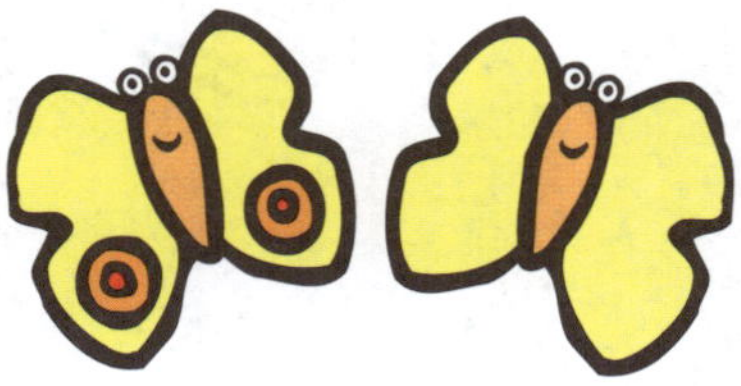

II Copy these numbers to match.

a 1 ____

b 2 ____

c 3 ____

d 4 ____

e 5 ____

f 6 ____

All about *9* and *10*

Here are the numbers **9** and **10**.

nine

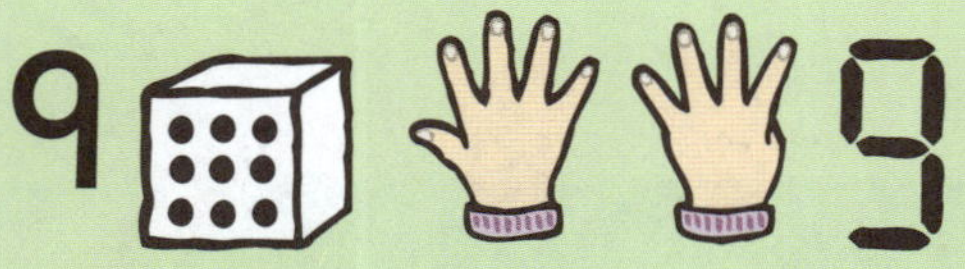

ten

I Count the spots on each T-shirt. Draw lines to join the T-shirts to the correct numbers.

II Draw lines to join 9 and 10 to their homes.

All about *0*

The number **0** shows **nothing**, or **zero**.

zero 0 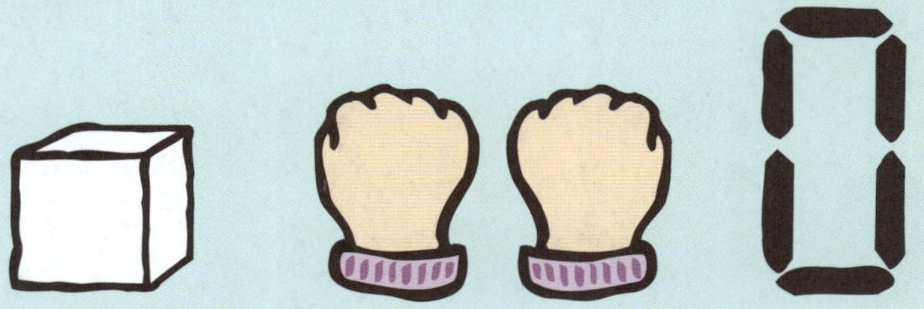

I Colour the boxes that have nothing in them.

II Draw lines to join the empty plates to the 0.

0

Counting to *10*

Count the stars and say the numbers out loud.

1 2 3 4 5 6 7 8 9 10

I **Count the marbles in each bag. Join them to the correct number.**

1 2 3 4 5 6 7 8 9 10

II **Draw some eggs in each box. Count how many there are.**

a

There are ________ eggs in this box.

b

There are ________ eggs in this box.

1 more

Count the birds on the branch.

Now there is **1 more**.

I **Count the caterpillars on a leaf. Draw caterpillars on the other leaf to show 1 more.**

a

b

c

II **Count the eggs in each nest. Join them in order.**

ANSWERS

Page 2

I a train
b doll
c kite
d boat
e car

II

Page 3

I

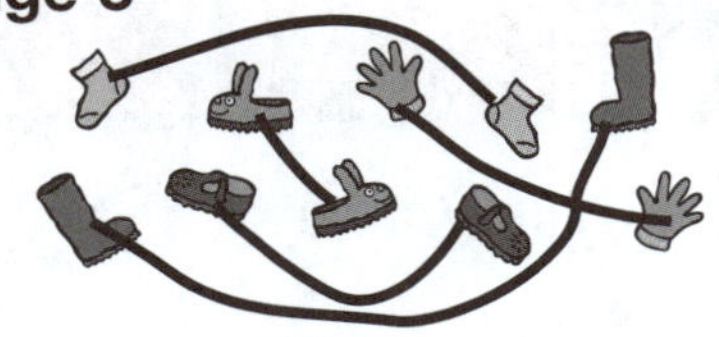

II Check patterns match on each pair.

Page 4

I

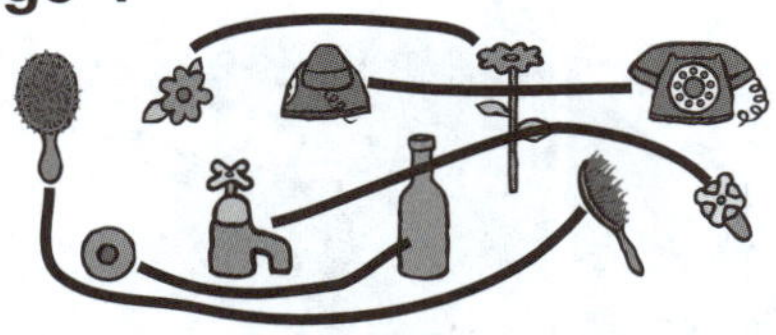

II The matching pairs are a and e; c and d; b and f.

Page 5

I

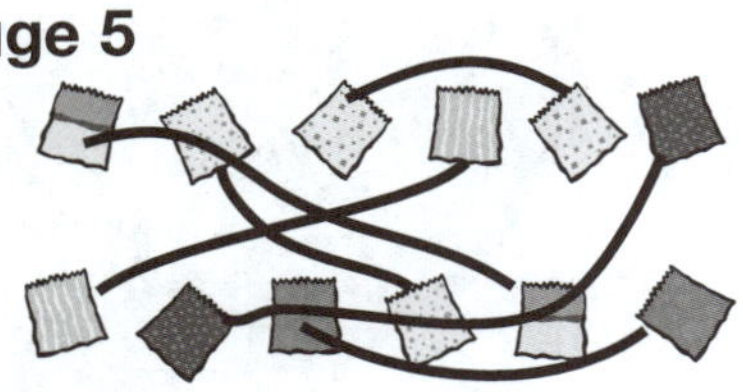

II Check the child has coloured the pairs correctly.

Page 6

I a

c

b

d

II a

b

c

Page 7

I Point to all the objects in each set.

II

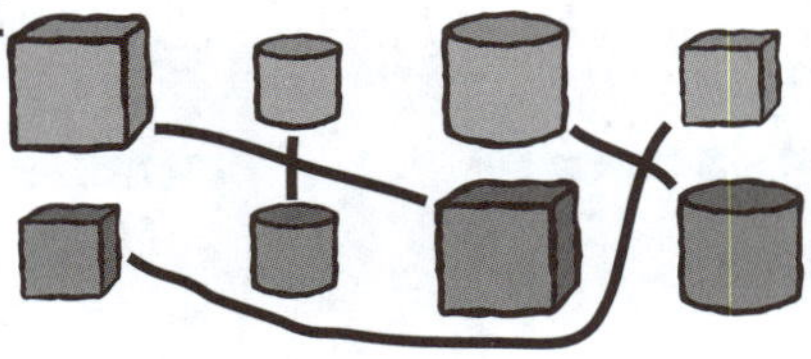

Page 8

I

II Check the pattern is a different pattern.

Page 9

I

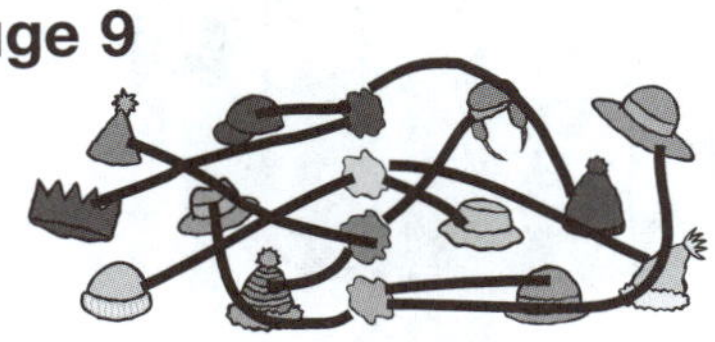

II

purple

green

orange

Page 10

I Point to spots, stripes, square and zig zag patterns.

II

Page 11

I a

b

II

Page 12

I a b c d

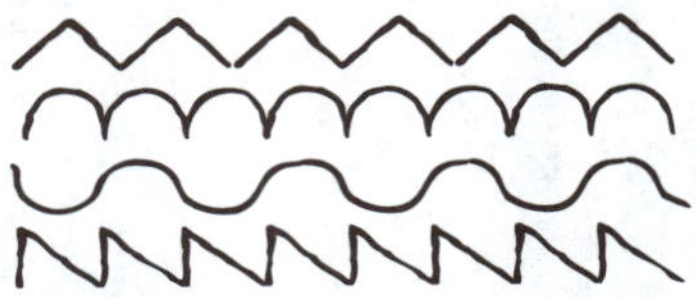

II a b c

Page 13

I

II a

b

Page 14

I red: c, d, e and g
blue: a, b and f

II a 4
b 3

Page 15

I

II Check child's drawing.

Page 16

I a c e b d f

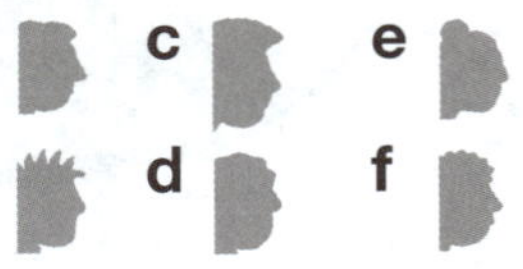

II a

b

c

Page 17

I

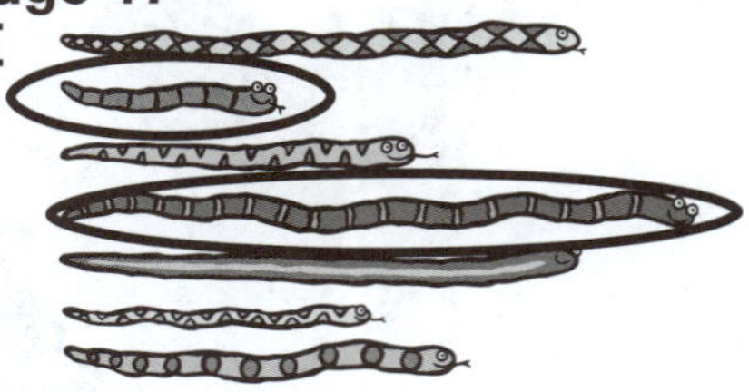

II a

b

Page 18

I

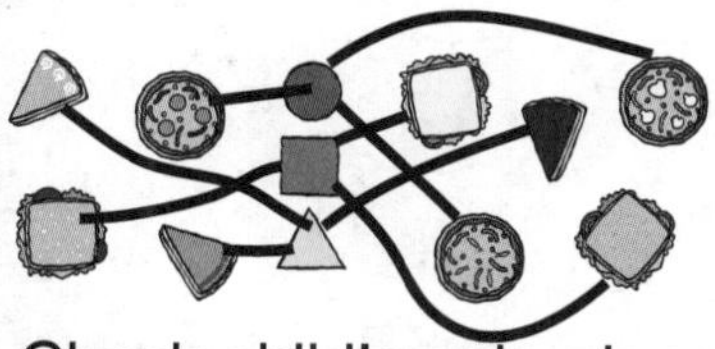

II Check child's colouring.

Page 19

I

II a 

b 

c 

Page 20

I

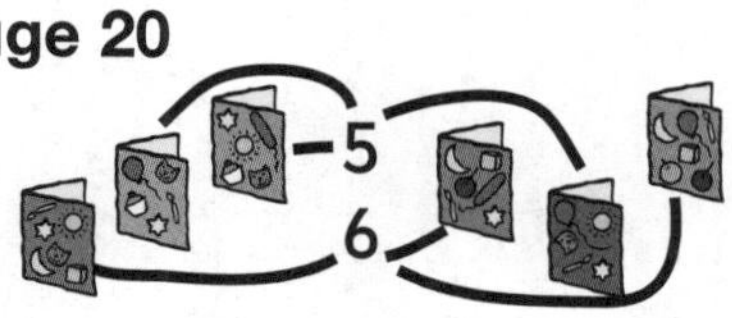

II a ••••• b ••••••

Page 21

I yellow: b, c and e
green: a, d and f

II a 6 b 7

Page 22

I Check child has coloured all the first pictures blue and the last red.

II

Page 23

I

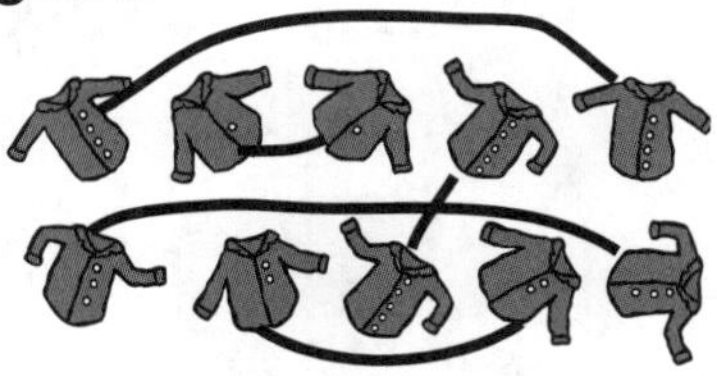

II a ••• d ••••
b • e ••
c •••••

Page 24

I

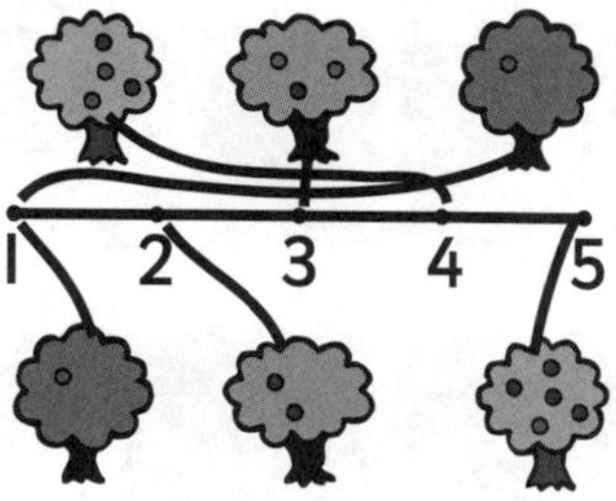

II a Draw one dot.
b Draw three dots.
c Draw two dots.
d Draw four dots.

Page 25

I Car 1 is green
Car 2 is red
Car 3 is blue
Car 4 is orange
Car 5 is yellow

II

Page 26

I Check child's writing.

II a • d ••••
b •• e •••••
c •••

Page 27

I

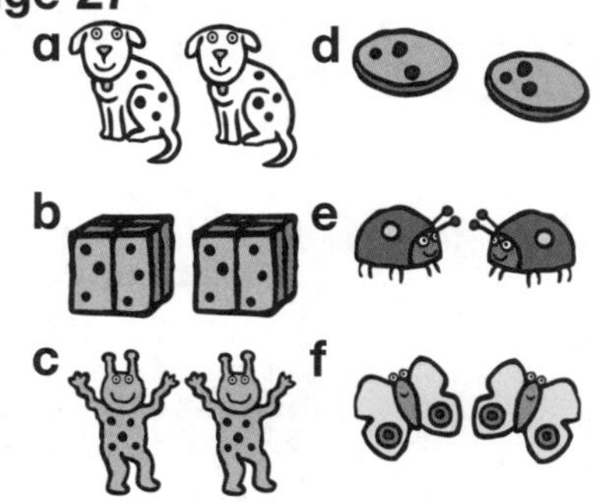

II Check that the child has written the numbers correctly.

Page 28

I

II

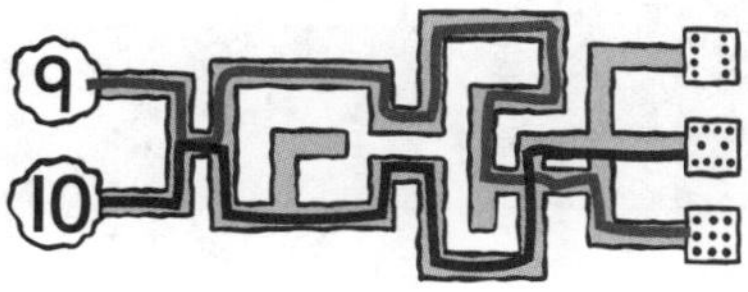

Page 29

I

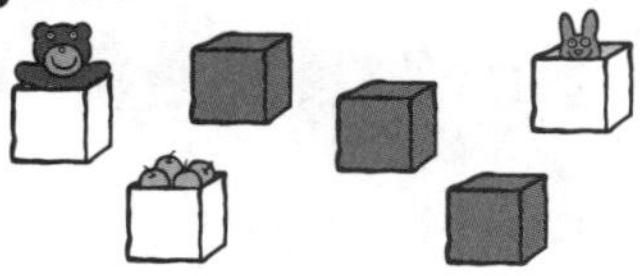

II

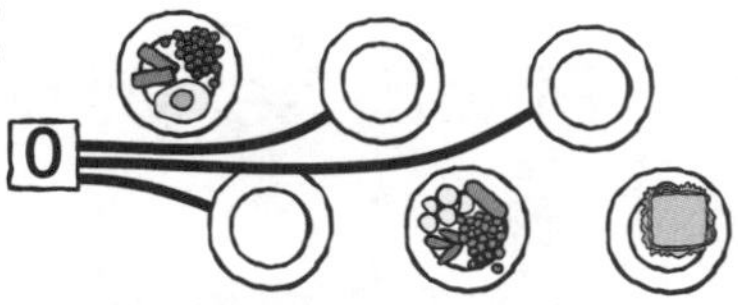

Page 30

I

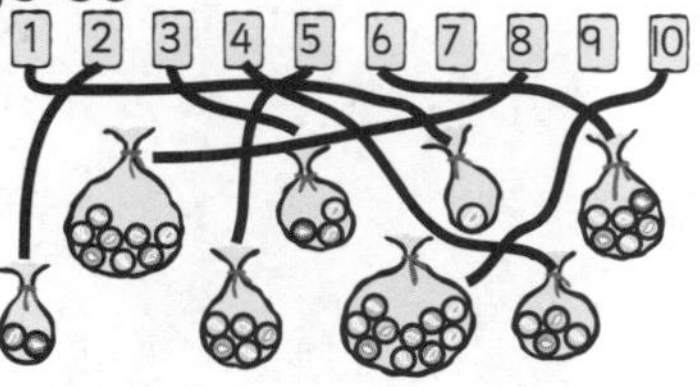

II Check the child's answers.

Page 31

I

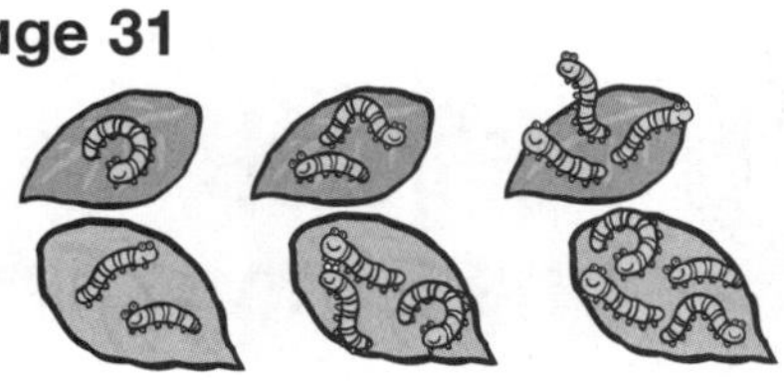

II

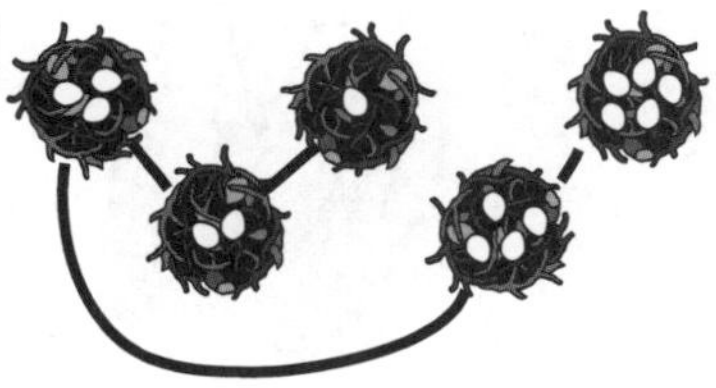

Sorting

You can sort objects by putting them into **sets**.

I Sort these in different ways.

a Find a set of forks.

b Find a set of red things.

c Find a set of small things.

d Find a set of knives.

II Where do these objects belong? Draw lines to join each one to the correct room.

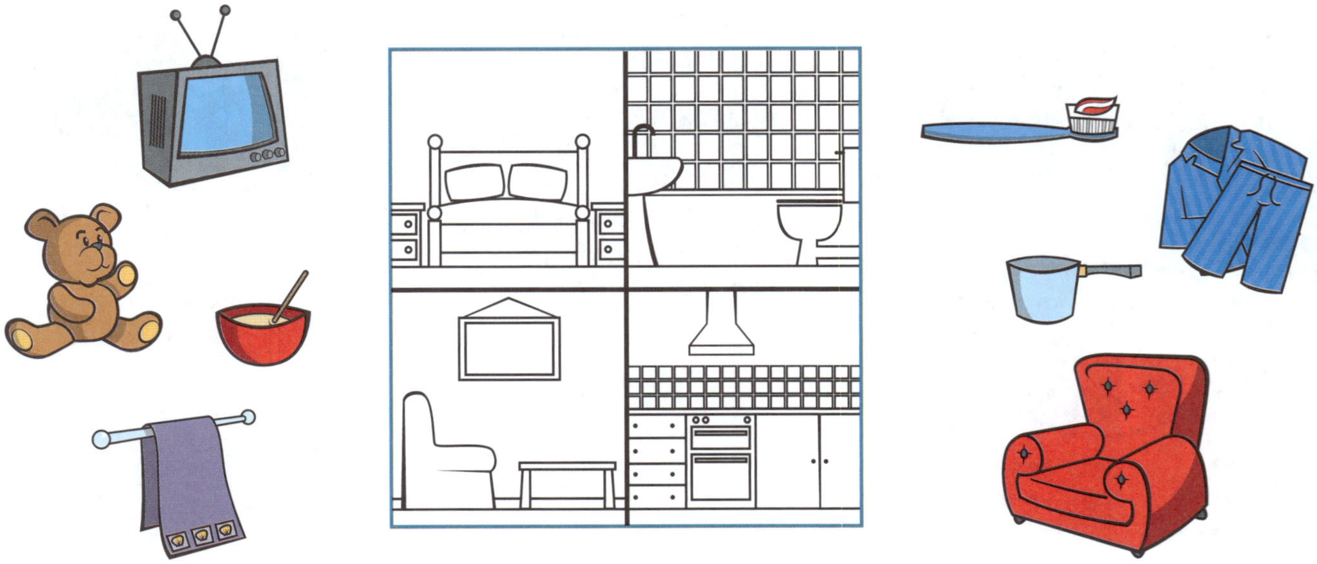

Matching pairs

A pair of objects is a set of two things.

Sometimes pairs match – they may **look the same**.

Sometimes pairs **go together**.

I Draw lines to join the matching pairs of shoes.

II Which pairs go together? Fill them in with the same colour.

Line patterns

Lines can be

straight...

...and **curved**.

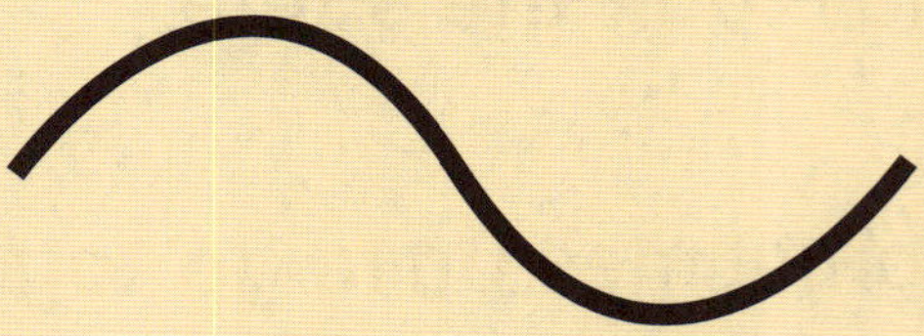

I **Draw over these lines.**

a 

b 

c 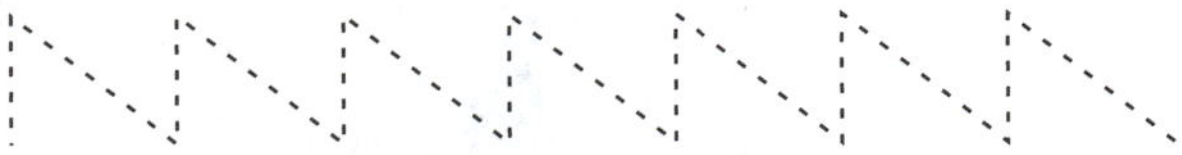

d 

e 

f 

g 

h 

II **Design your own line pattern. Draw it as a border for this picture.**

Matching shapes

Look at the shapes of objects around you.

See what makes them the **same** and what makes them **different**.

straight lines

points

curved lines

I Draw lines to join each rocket to its shadow.

II Cross out the odd one in each row.

a

b

c

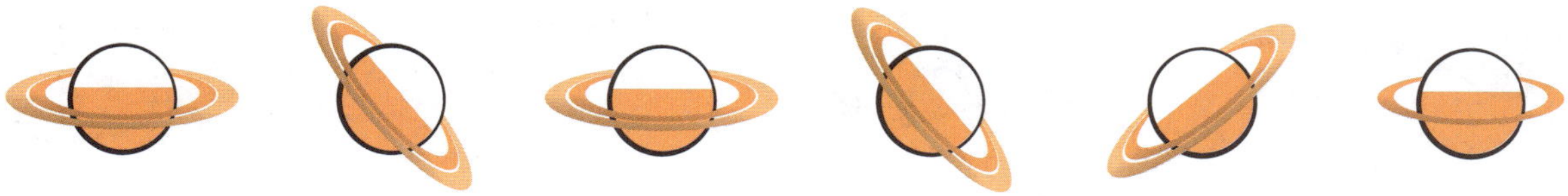

Comparing sizes

Compare the **size** of things.

smallest → → largest

I Tick the largest in each set. Cross out the smallest in each set.

a

c

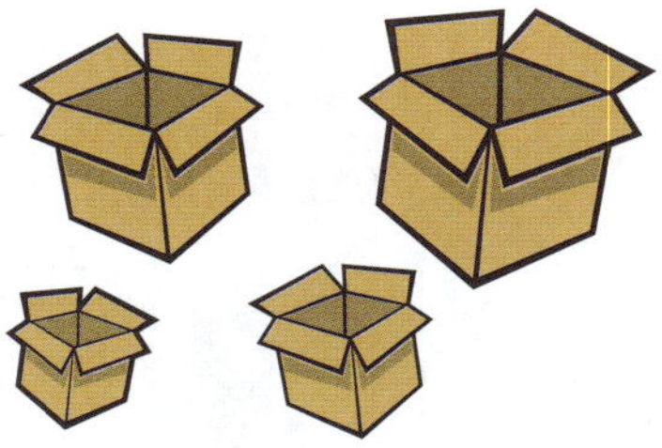

e

b

d

f

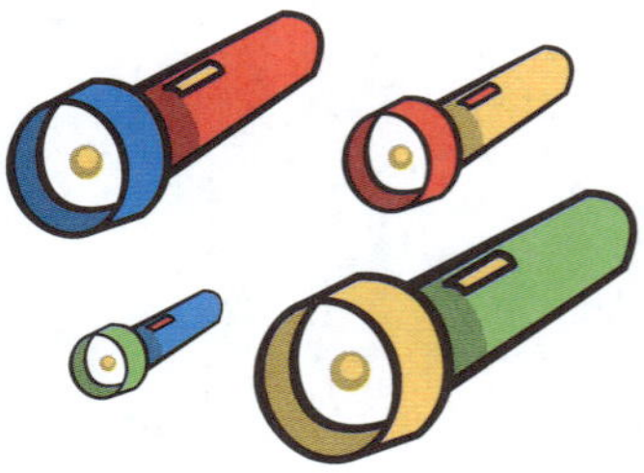

II Draw lines to join these parcels in order of size. Start with the smallest.

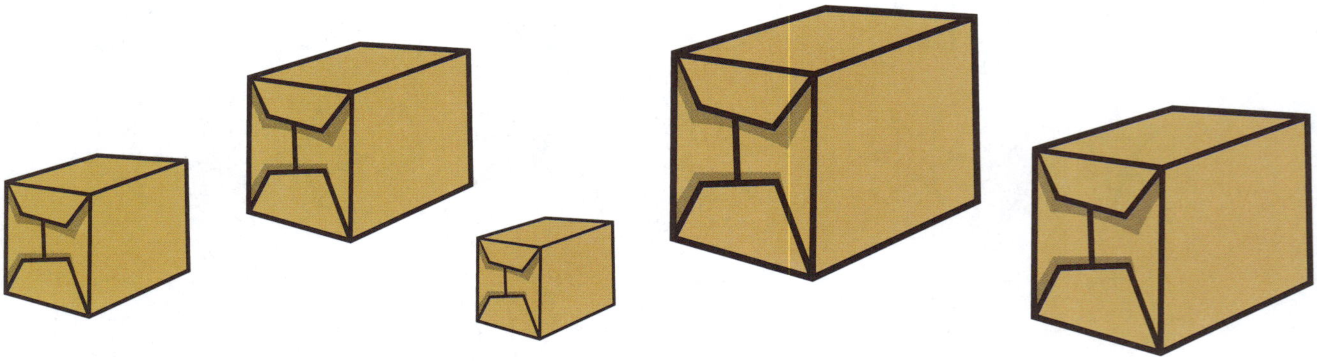

Numbers to *3*

Talk about numbers **1**, **2** and **3**.

I Draw lines to join the numbers to their matching sets.

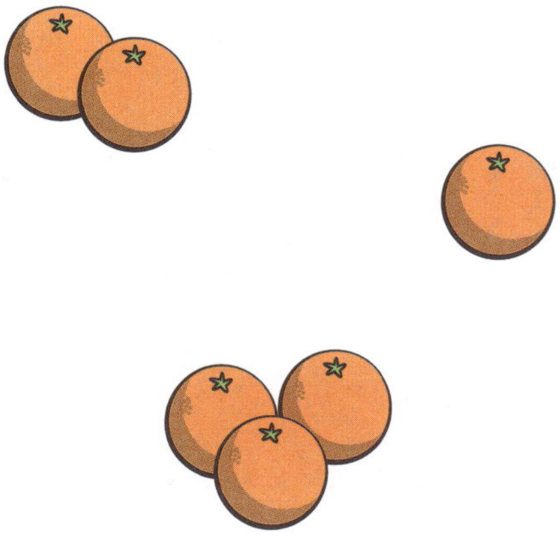

1
2
3

II Cross out the odd one in each set.

a

c

b

d

Writing numbers to *3*

Practise **writing** these numbers.

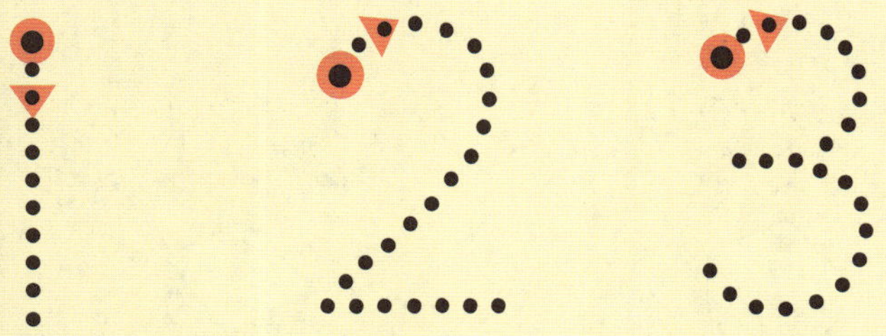

Follow the shape of the numbers with your finger.

I **Write these numbers. Start at the red dots.**

a

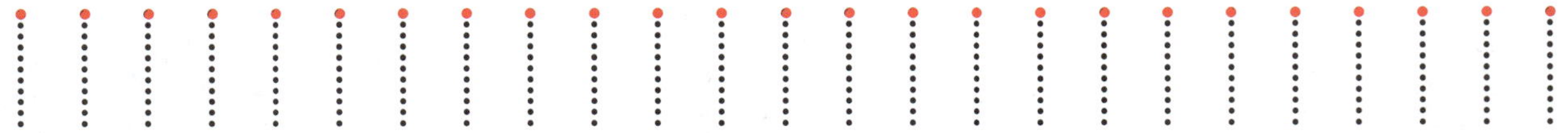

b

c

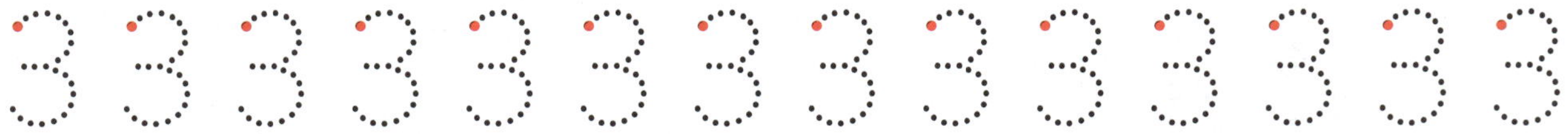

II **Write the number on each card. Draw the same number of candles on each cake.**

a

b

c

Recognising shapes

Look at the **shapes** of things around you.

I Find these shapes in the big picture. Colour them to match.

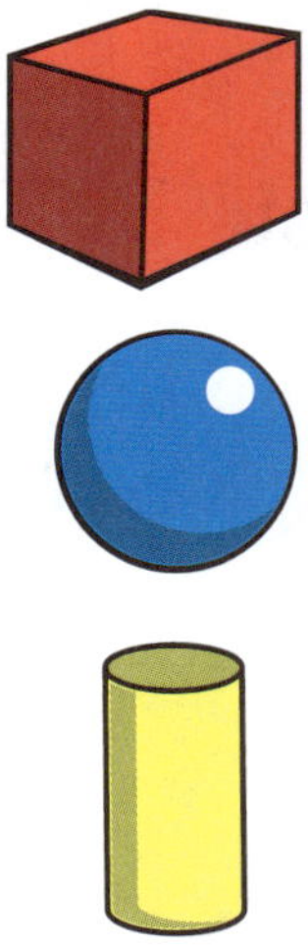

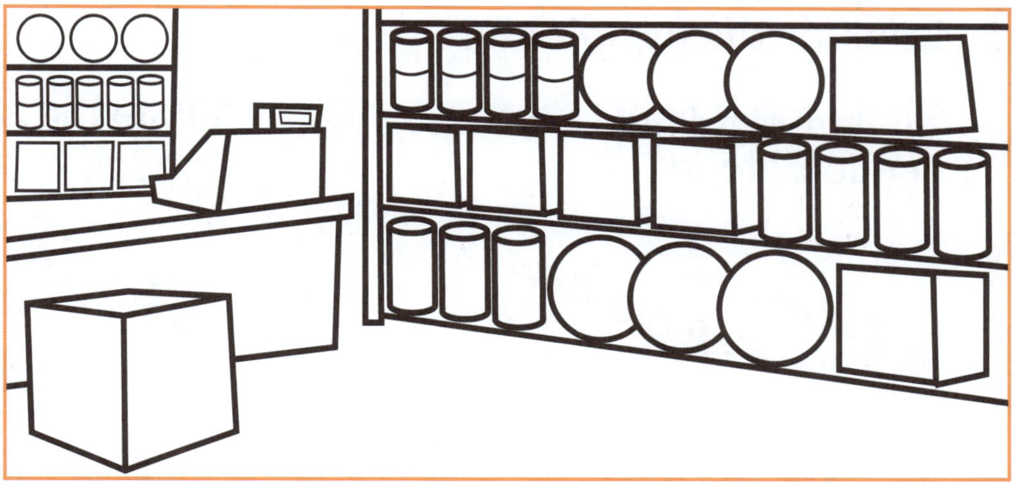

II Draw lines to join each lid to the correct box. Colour to match.

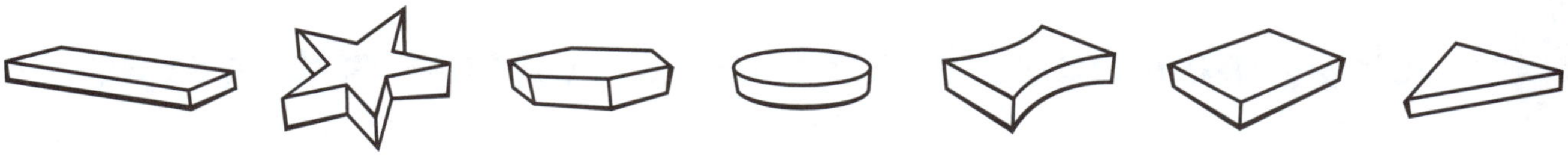

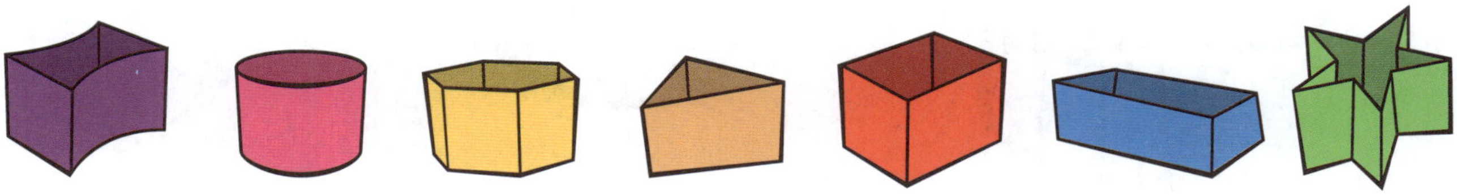

Comparing lengths

Compare the **lengths** of different objects.

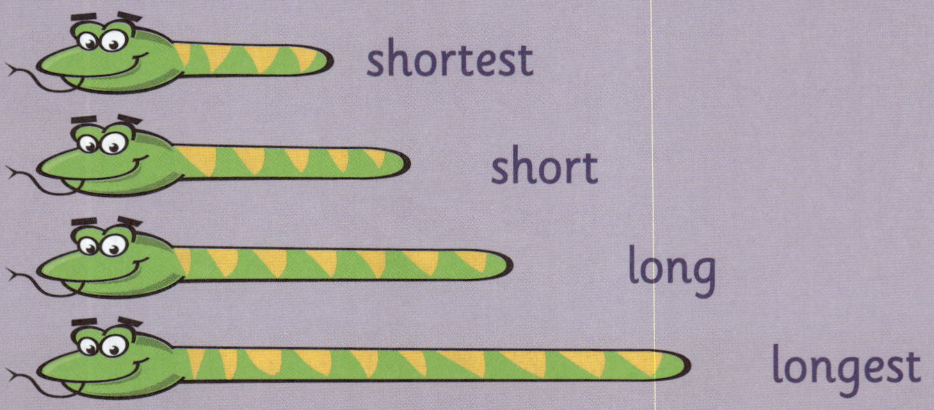

I Look at these objects.

Circle the longest in each group.

a

b

Circle the shortest in each group.

c

d

II Colour the longest scarf blue. Colour the shortest scarf red.

a

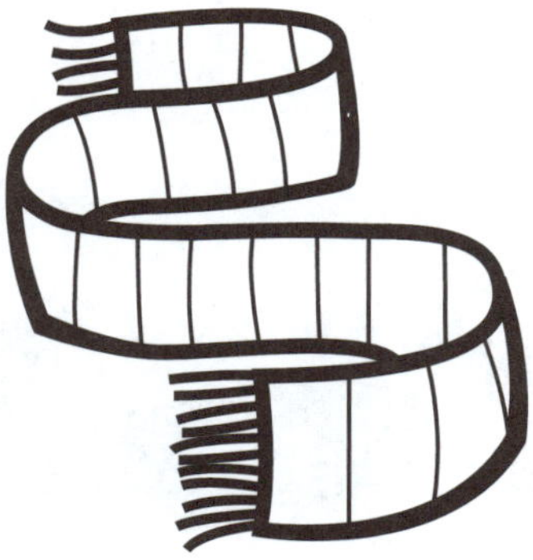

b

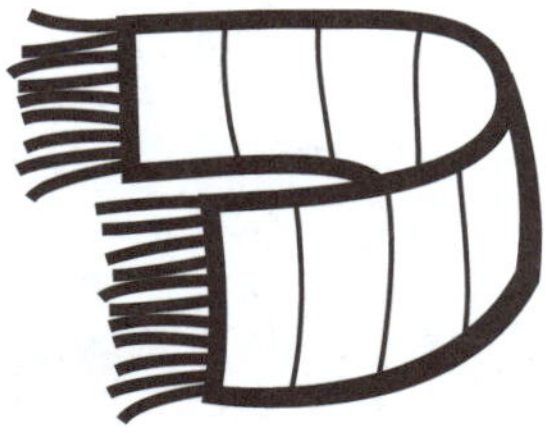

c

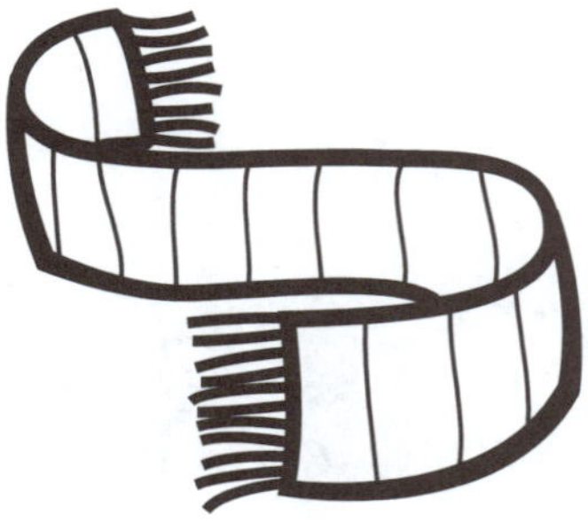

Numbers 4, 5 and 6

Talk about numbers **4**, **5** and **6**.

4 

5 

6 

I Draw juggling balls to match the number below each clown.

a b c

3 4 5 6

II Draw lines to join each card to the correct number.

4 5 6

Writing numbers to *6*

Practise **writing** these numbers.

4	5	6

2 3 4	2 3 4 5	2 3 4 5 6

I **Write these numbers. Start at the red dots.**

a 4 4 4 4 4 4 4 4 4 4 4 4 4 4

b 5 5 5 5 5 5 5 5 5 5 5 5 5 5

c 6 6 6 6 6 6 6 6 6 6 6 6 6 6

II **Write these numbers. Draw the same number of spots on each balloon.**

1 2 3 4 5 6

Counting to *5*

When you count objects, the **last number** you say tells you how many there are.

I Draw lines to join the matching kites.

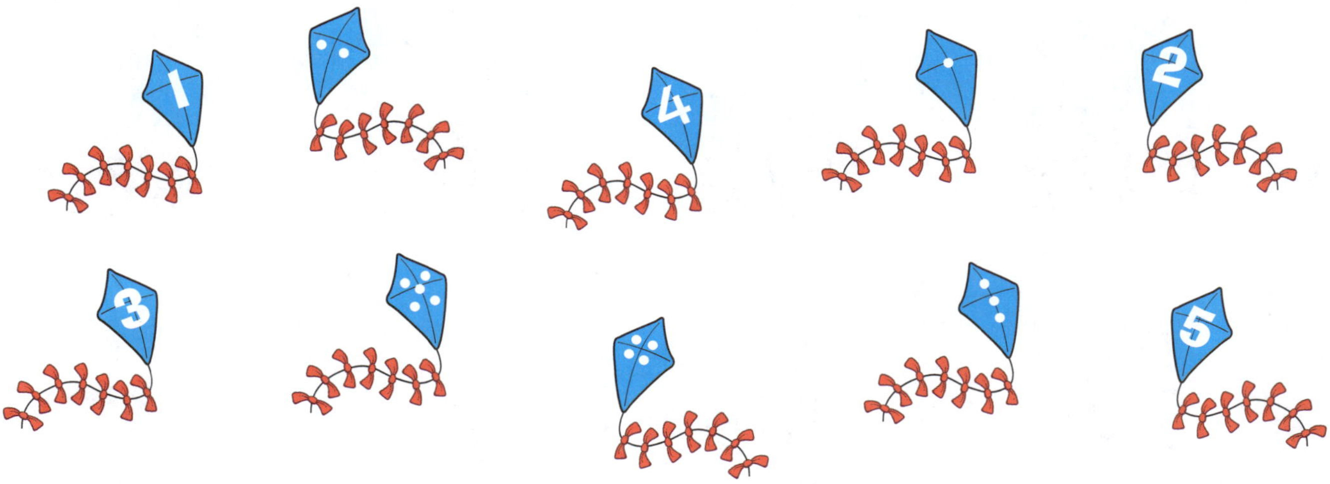

II Count each set of birds. Write down the number.

a

c

e

b

d

f

Ordering events

We often do things in a certain **order**.

I Write the numbers 1, 2, 3 and 4 to show the order of each activity.

a

b

II Draw a line to show when you do these things.

morning

afternoon

evening

Numbers *7, 8* and *9*

Think about the numbers **7**, **8** and **9**.

I Draw the right number of spots on each ladybird.

a b c

7 8 9

II Circle the odd one out in each row.

a

b

c

Writing numbers to *9*

Practise **writing** these numbers.

7  1 2 3 4 5 6 7

8 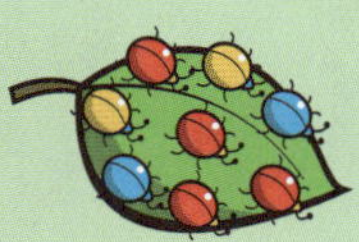 1 2 3 4 5 6 7 8

9 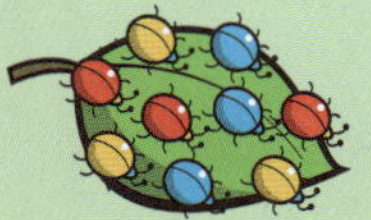 1 2 3 4 5 6 7 8 9

I **Write these numbers. Start at the red dots.**

a 7 7 7 7 7 7 7 7 7 7 7 7 7 7

b 8 8 8 8 8 8 8 8 8 8 8 8 8 8

c 9 9 9 9 9 9 9 9 9 9 9 9 9 9

II **Write the numbers. Colour the stars to match each number.**

a 1 

b 2 

c 3 

d 4 

e 5 

f 6 

g 7 

h 8 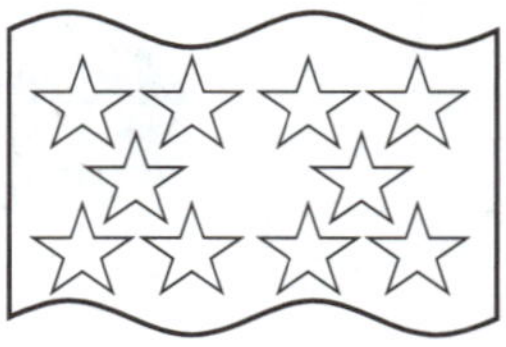

i 9 

Patterns

Shapes and **colours** can make different patterns.

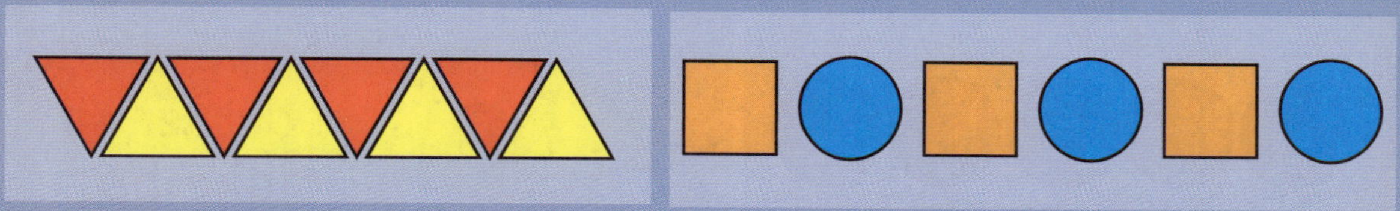

I **Trace over these patterns. Continue each one.**

II **Copy each shape below. Colour each line to make a pattern.**

a

b

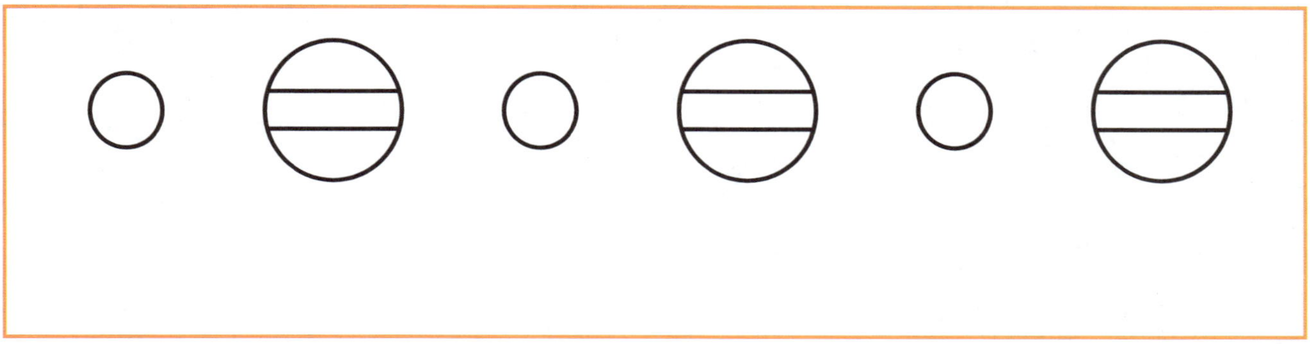

Pennies

We count pennies to make **totals**.

5 pennies add together to make 5p.

I Count the pennies. Write the totals in each purse.

a

b

c

d

II Count each row of pennies. Colour the matching label.

a

2p

1p

3p

b

2p

1p

3p

c

2p

4p

3p

Zero *0* and *10*

Practise writing **0** and **10**.

0 1 2 3 4 5 6 7 8 9 10

I Write over these numbers. Start at the red dots.

a

b

II Follow each path to join 0 and 10 to the correct fields of sheep.

Counting to *10*

Count the flowers and say the numbers out loud.

I **Draw lines to join each set of frogs to the correct number.**

II **Draw some fish in these ponds. Count how many you have drawn.**

a

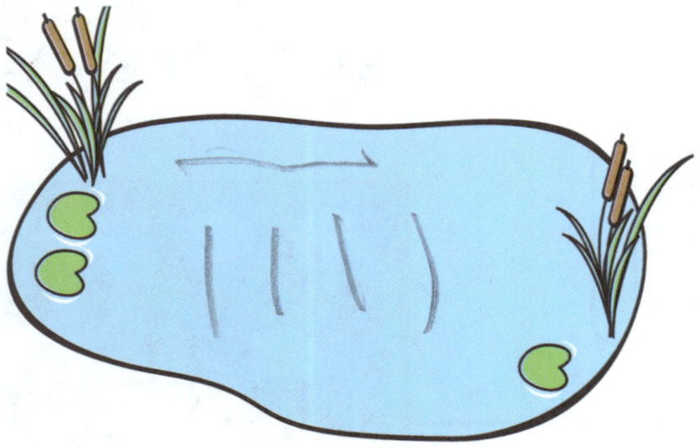

I have drawn 5 fish.

b

I have drawn 1 fish.

Recognising numbers

Try to learn these **numbers** and their **names**.

1	2	3	4	5	6	7	8	9	10
one	two	three	four	five	six	seven	eight	nine	ten

I Draw the correct number of spots on each kite.

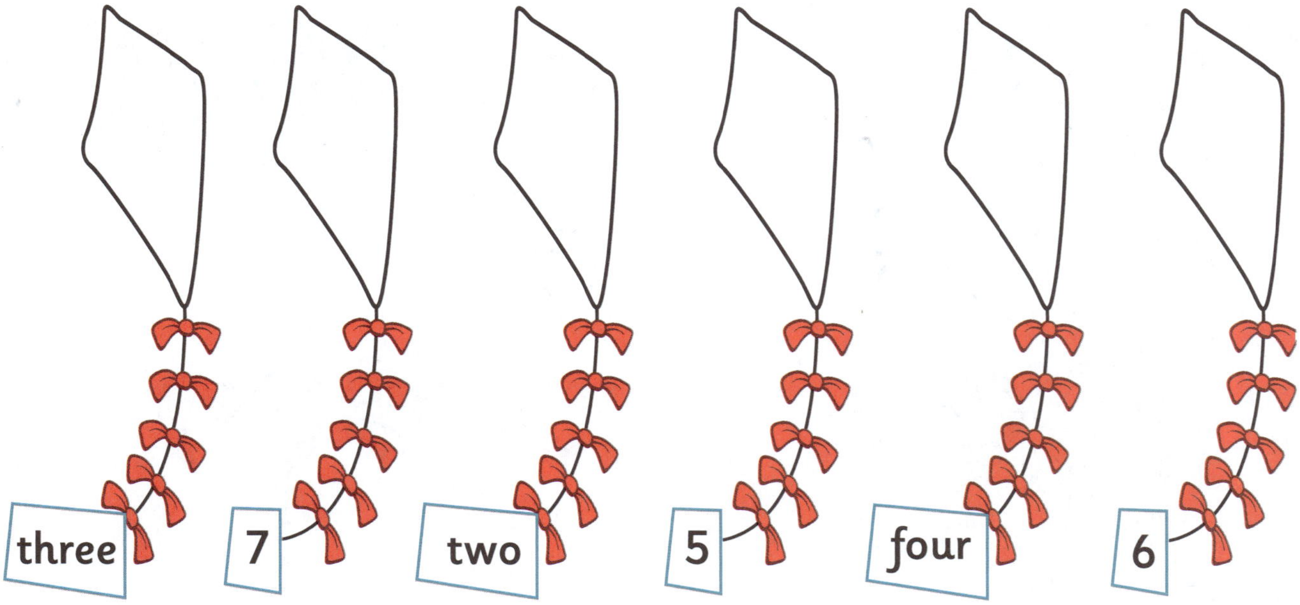

II Cross out the odd one on each line.

a

b

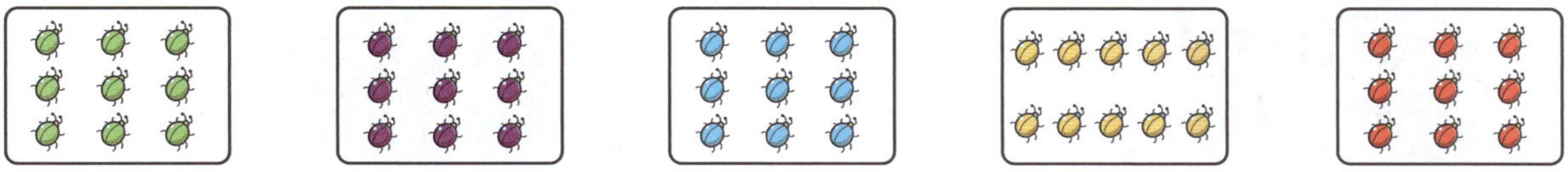

c

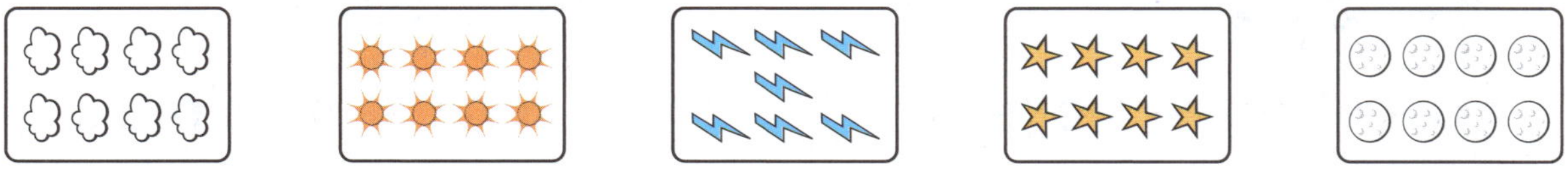

1 more

There is **1 more** ball in each row.

I Draw 1 more balloon in each group. Write how many balloons there are altogether.

a

☐

c

☐

b

☐

d

☐

II Draw one more candle on each cake. Complete the sentence.

a

☐ and 1 more makes ☐

b

☐ and 1 more makes ☐

Recognising coins

These are some of the coins we use.

10p is worth 10 pennies.

I Cross out the odd one in each purse.

a

b

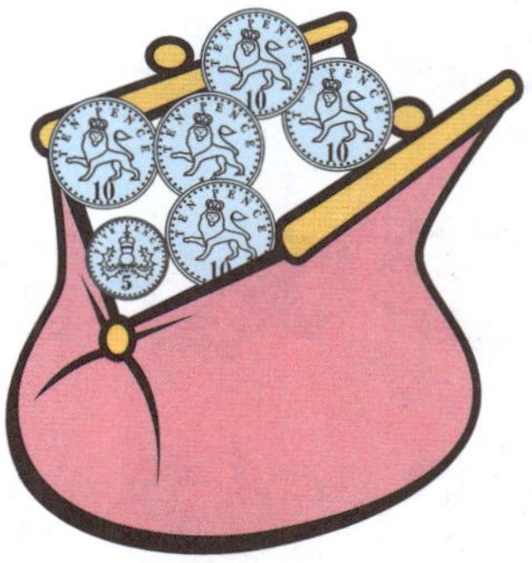

c

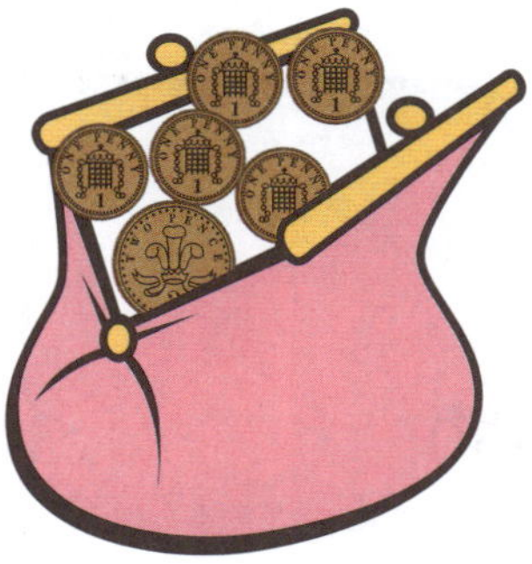

d

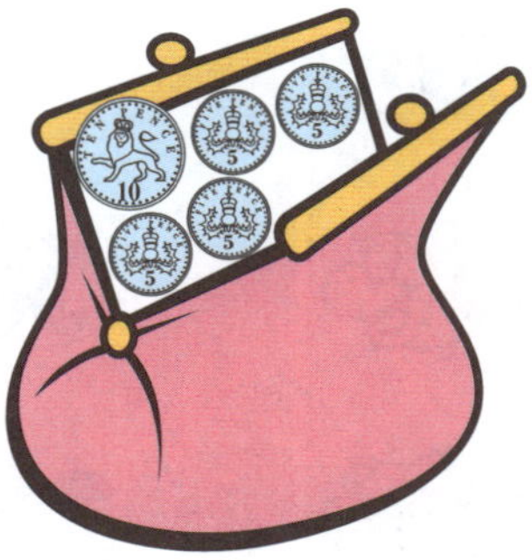

e

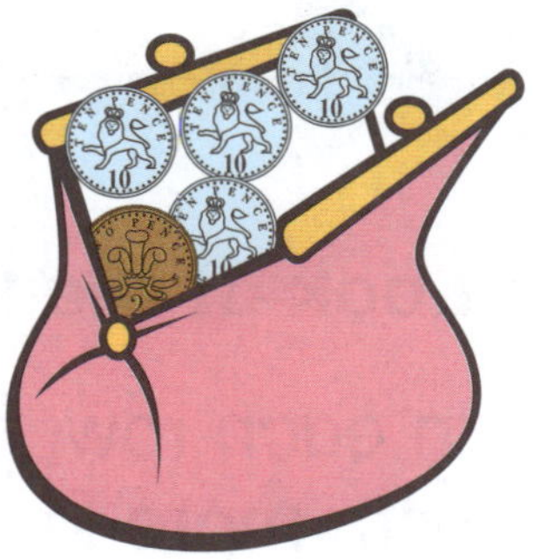

f

II Write the totals for each of these.

a

b

c

d

Comparing amounts

The words **more**, **fewer** and **same** are used to compare amounts.

- There are **more** blue fish than red fish.
- There are **fewer** red fish than yellow fish.
- There are the **same** number of blue fish as yellow fish.

I Look at the fish.

a In each row, tick the fish with **more** spots.

b In each row, tick the fish with **fewer** spots.

II Look at each set of fish. Draw bubbles by the second fish.

a Draw **more** bubbles.

b Draw **fewer** bubbles.

c Draw the **same** number of bubbles.

Naming shapes

Try to learn the names of these shapes. Count the **number of sides** of each shape.

I Colour the shapes in the picture to match the colour of the shapes above.

II Look at these shapes. Count the shapes.

a There are ☐ 3-sided shapes. **b** There are ☐ 4-sided shapes.

Ordering numbers

Try to learn the **order** of numbers.

1	2	3	4	5	6	7	8	9	10
1st	2nd	3rd	4th	5th	6th	7th	8th	9th	10th
first	second	third	fourth	fifth	sixth	seventh	eighth	ninth	tenth

I Draw lines to join these in order.

a

b

II These boats are in a race. Colour the 1st red. Colour the 2nd blue. Colour the 3rd yellow.

Finding totals

Count each set to find a total.

4 and 3 makes 7 altogether.

I Count the creatures to find each total.

a

☐ and ☐ makes ☐

b

☐ and ☐ makes ☐

c

☐ and ☐ makes ☐

d

☐ and ☐ makes ☐

II Draw 3 more spots on each bear. How many are there now on each bear?

a

There are ☐ spots on this bear.

b

There are ☐ spots on this bear.

c

There are ☐ spots on this bear.

Counting patterns

Counting patterns help you to work out **missing numbers**. Say these numbers out loud.

1 2 3   5   7

The missing numbers are 4 and 6.

I Write the missing numbers.

a 3, 4, 5, 6, ___, ___, 9

b 10, 9, 8, 7, ___, ___, ___

c 5, 6, 7, 8, ___, 10, ___

d 12, 11, 10, ___, ___, ___, 6

II How far can you count past 10? Read these numbers and colour the ones you know.

6 7 8 9 10 11 12 13 14 15 16 17 18 19 20

Adding

You **add** things by putting them together and finding a **total**.

and

makes

I Write the missing numbers. Add them up.

a 

and 

makes ☐

b 

and 
makes ☐

c 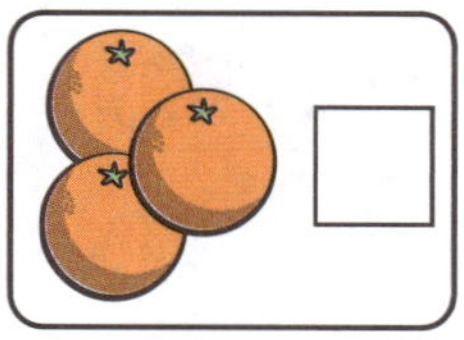
and 
makes ☐

II Join together the dominoes with matching totals.

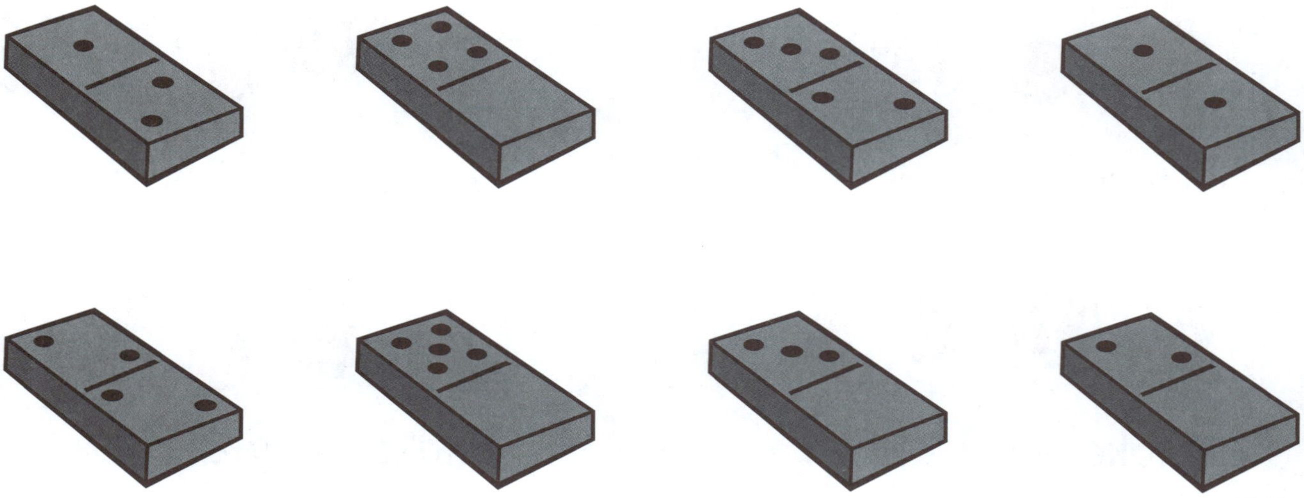

Taking away

When you **take 1 away**, there is 1 fewer.

5 take away 1 leaves 4.

I Cross 1 out and write what is left.

a

4 take away 1 is ☐

b

5 take away 1 is ☐

c

3 take away 1 is ☐

d

6 take away 1 is ☐

II Cross 2 out and write what is left.

a

3 take away 2 is ☐

b

4 take away 2 is ☐

c

5 take away 2 is ☐

d

6 take away 2 is ☐

O'clock time

When the minute hand points to the 12 it shows an **o'clock** time.

The hour hand is pointing to 4.
This clock shows 4 o'clock or 4.00.

I Write these times.

a

☐ o'clock

c

☐ o'clock

e

☐ o'clock

b

☐ o'clock

d

☐ o'clock

f

☐ o'clock

II Join the clocks which show the same time.

ANSWERS

Page 2
I Check child's sorting.
II
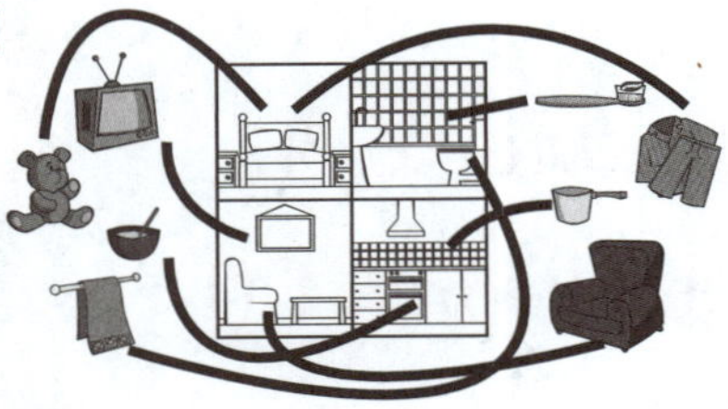

Page 3
I

II
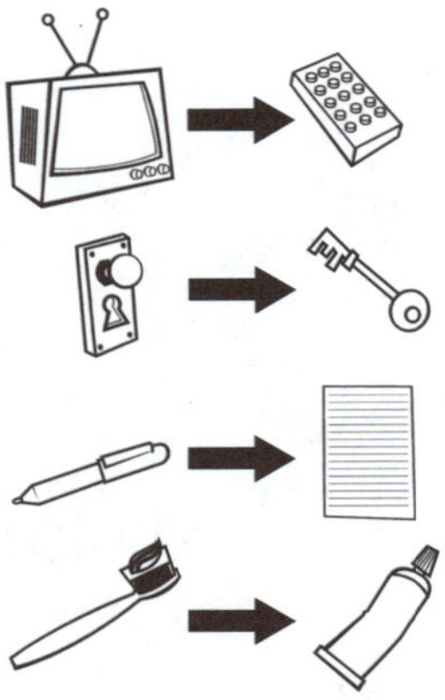

Page 4
I a–h
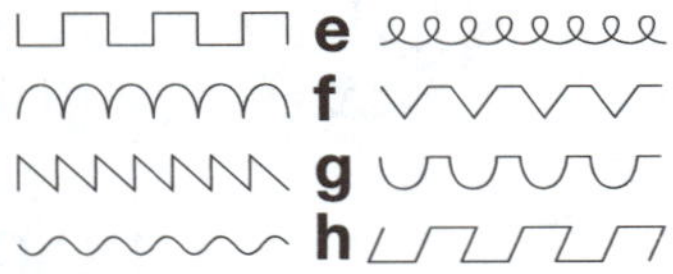

II Check child's line pattern.

Page 5
I

II
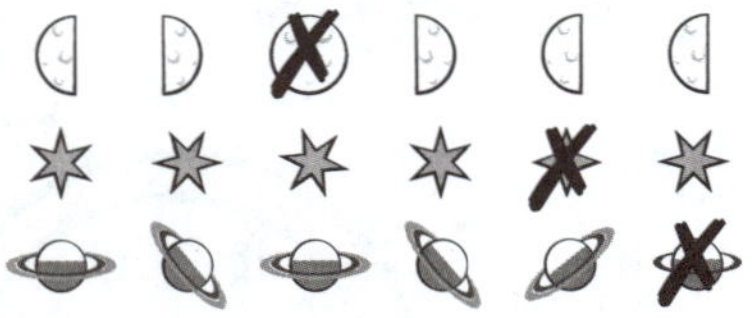

Page 6
I a, b, c, d, e, f
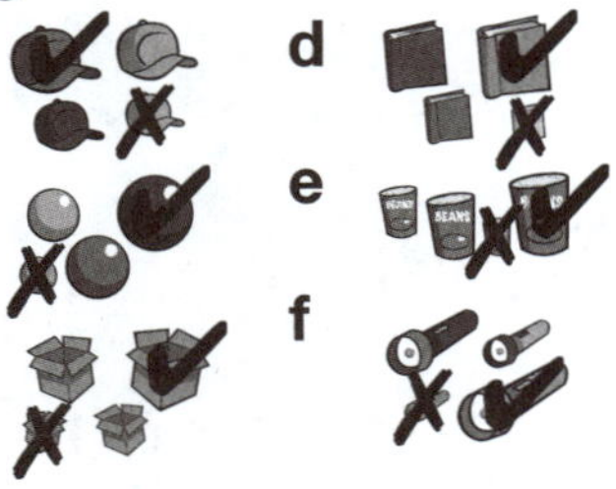

II
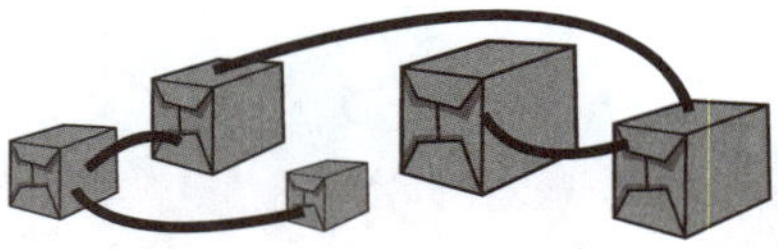

Page 7
I
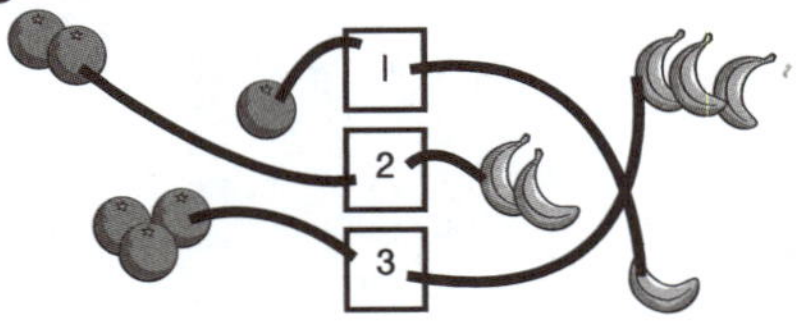

II a, b, c, d
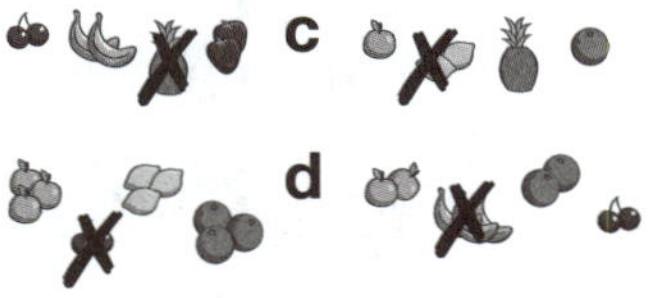

Page 8
I a 111111111111111111111
b 22222222222222
c 33333333333333

II

Page 9
I Check the shapes are coloured correctly.
II
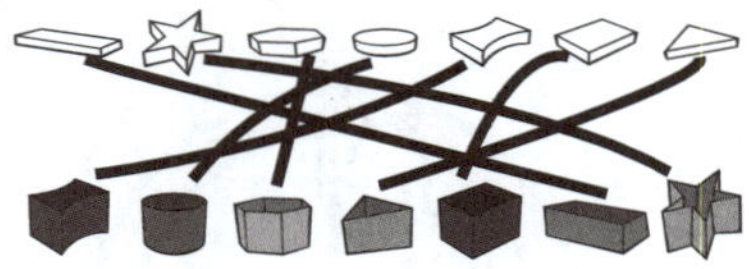

Page 10
I a, b, c, d
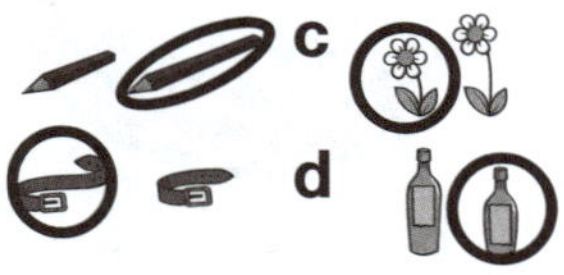

II Check **a** is coloured blue and **b** is coloured red.

Page 11
I a, b, c

II
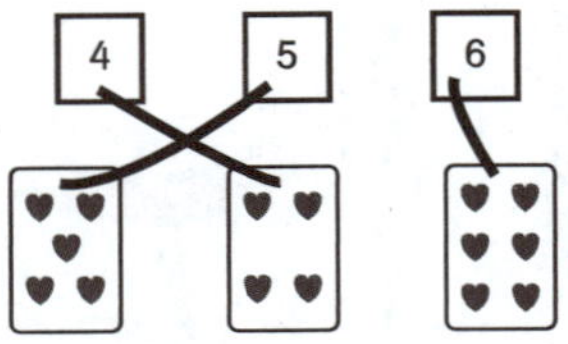

Page 12
I a 44444444444444
b 55555555555555
c 66666666666666

II

Page 13
I
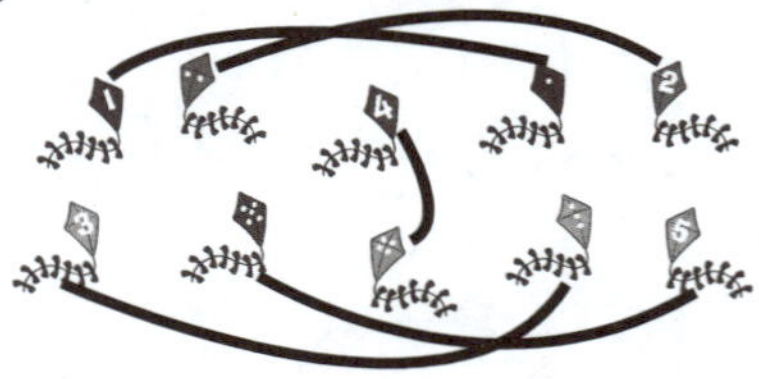

II a 4 c 3 e 5
b 1 d 2 f 4

Page 14
I a 3, 1, 4, 2
b 1, 3, 4, 2

II
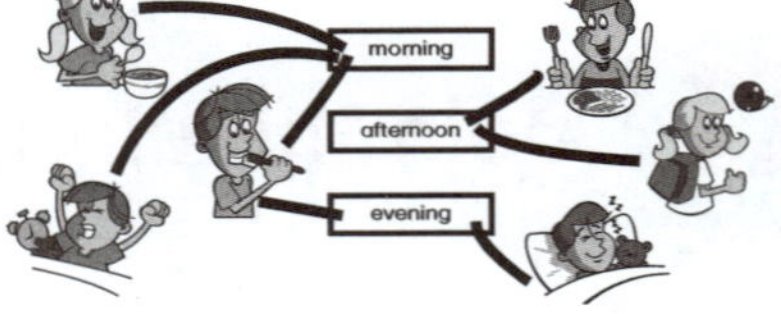

Page 15
I a, b, c

II a, b, c